Achieving "PEACE OF MIND" in Life, Business, and Sports

Business-Minded, Modern Day Individuals

By Mike Ross

Achieving Peace of Mind in Life, Business, and Sports

Copyright 2025 – Mike Ross

All rights reserved.

Printed in the United States of America

No part of this book may be used or reproduced, stored in a retrieval system, or transmitted in any form or by any means, electronic, mechanical, photocopying, recording, or otherwise, without the prior written permission of the author except in the case of brief quotations embodied in critical articles or reviews.

Paperback Edition ISBN – 978-1-949802-47-4

Published by Black Pawn Press

FIRST EDITION

Preface

In this book, I will guide you on the path to achieving peace of mind in every aspect of life—be it personal, professional, or beyond. Together, we will explore the essential steps, principles, and practices that lead to this state of inner calm. Through shared experiences, insights, and actionable strategies, I aim to provide you with a clear roadmap to cultivate balance, fulfillment, and tranquility.

Peace of mind is not simply a goal to be achieved; it is a way of being—a journey of self-discovery, preparation, and intentional living. By the end of this book, you will have the tools and understanding to embrace this journey, empowering you to navigate life's challenges with grace and find lasting contentment in the moments that matter most.

In today's fast-paced and interconnected world, the role of a leader has evolved dramatically. Leadership in the Digital Age requires a balance between driving success and maintaining personal well-being. This book, "Peace of Mind in Life, Business and Sports," is a culmination of over 30 years of my experiences as an entrepreneur, father, spouse, coach, and an athlete. It is my sincere hope that through these pages you'll find a pathway to achieving not only success, but also peace of mind; a valuable asset in every facet of life.

Throughout my career, I've witnessed countless leaders strive for success, often at the expense of their personal well-being. The relentless pursuit of growth and achievement can lead to stress, burnout, and ultimately, a lack of fulfillment. Twenty years later, the kids are in college and they realized what they missed out on –with much regret. Personally, my schedule each week, while the kids were growing up, was family, school events, working out, and then, I would pencil in my company tasks/appointments. Surprisingly, this process always worked out and I was fulfilled! Recognizing this, I have crafted each chapter of this book with step-by-step guidelines aimed at reaching the next level on your road to achieving peace of mind.

Whether you're an entrepreneur, coach, business owner, corporate leader, parent, or spouse, this book is for you. It serves as a roadmap to help you harmonize your professional, athletic and personal life, enabling you to lead with clarity, purpose, and tranquility. By sharing real-life experiences and insights, my goal is to empower you to become a more effective leader in the digital age—one that not only achieves success but also finds enduring peace of mind.

"Impossible is just a big word thrown around by small people who find it easier to live in the world they've been given than to explore the power they have to change it. Impossible is not a fact. It's an opinion. Impossible is not a declaration. It's a dare. Impossible is potential. Impossible is temporary. Impossible is nothing."
-Muhammed Ali

Introduction

Navigating the Modern Business Landscape

In contemporary business and athletic environments, professionals—both male and female—are constantly navigating an ever-changing landscape of challenges and opportunities. The pressures of entrepreneurship, sports at a high level and leadership demand not only expertise and determination but also emotional intelligence and adaptability. Today's business-minded individuals must find innovative ways to integrate personal well-being with professional success, ensuring that each facet of life contributes positively to the other. This book aims to provide the tools and insights needed to achieve this balance. It emphasizes the importance of self-care, mindfulness, and continuous learning as critical components of leadership. Whether you are launching a startup, accelerating a corporate career, playing sports on collegiate, professional or Olympic level or juggling multiple roles, embracing these principles can help you thrive amid the complexities of modern day life, business sand sports.

The Role of Mentorship in Leadership

As a leader, one of the most impactful contributions you can make is investing time and resources in developing young talent. Talented young individuals possess fresh perspectives and innovative approaches to problem-solving, but often need guidance to channel their potential effectively. By prioritizing mentorship and fostering an environment of growth, you create opportunities for these emerging leaders to learn and thrive. Encourage them to tackle challenges head-on, provide constructive feedback, and guide them to set personal and professional goals. In doing so, you not only help them ascend to the next level but also build a more dynamic and resilient team. Empowering the next generation of leaders ensures continuity and strengthens the overall success of your organization.

Thank you for embarking on this journey with me. May this book inspire and guide you towards a leadership style that embraces both achievement and serenity.

Mike Ross

LinkedIn: Mike Ross

Instagram: Connextionspro and additionbuildingdesign

Acknowledgments

This project is a sum total of what I have learned as an entrepreneur since I was 12-years-old, working six jobs, attending school, and playing sports year-round.

My wife, Barbara, is the person who pushed me to complete this book to share with others how to achieve success and ultimately "peace of mind." Thank you Barbara also for showing me the importance of listening to others perspectives, as she has made me say so many times "I am so glad I asked you."

Judith A. Moose, my manager, for spearheading the publishing of this book.

My three brothers, Curt, Greg, and Gary, for driving me to be successful in everything I do. Our competitiveness every night with dad in the backyard helped shape my determination to never give up or stop striving to get better.

My employees: who inspire me to always be the best leader through open communication and transparency. You have taught me to be innovative, and how to drive the team to success.

My athletes who I have coached: thank you for so many great memories and the experience of winning and bouncing back from defeat.

My teammates: thank you for the camaraderie, pushing me to be the best and the importance of all of us doing our jobs for the betterment of the team.

My coaches in baseball, basketball, football, and track: thanks for pushing me to be tough, resilience, never quit, know the rules and how to be a great teammate.

My three daughters, Christine, Laura, and Jami, for inspiring me to understand what being a great dad takes: making sure you ALWAYS know how much I love you, and to ALWAYS give you my time each day, even if it's only five minutes.

Mom and Dad, Norm and Gloria, for being the most influential people in my life, and for teaching me sacrifice, love, teamwork, and the special importance of FAMILY.

Conclusion

The knowledge shared within these pages is a testament to years of dedication and experience, a roadmap for those seeking success and peace of mind in life, business and sports. May this book not only inspire but also empower you to lead with purpose, blending achievement with tranquility.

As we conclude this journey, let us embrace the passion that fuels our ambitions and the clarity that guides our paths.

Contents

1. What is Peace of Mind in Life, Business, and Sports — 17
2. If You Don't Ask, You Won't Get — 21
3. Overcoming Mistakes – Preventative — 26
4. Strategy: Outmaneuvering Any Rival — 33
5. The Art of "Negotiating" — 39
6. Integrity Across All Realms — 44
7. Goal Setting — 49
8. The Five Choices in Everything We Do — 52
9. Starting is Very Important…Finishing is Crucial — 56
10. Leadership – The Essence of Effectiveness — 61
11. Mentorship — 69
12. The Power of Perseverance — 73
13. The Essence of Family — 78
14. Embracing Failure as a Stepping Stone to Success — 86
15. Accountability — 90
16. Don't Waste Energy — 97
17. The Benefits of a Great Partner — 104
18. Living a Healthy Life — 111
19. Listening to Others' Perspective — 119

20. Problem Solving – The Key to the NEXT Level	124
21. Embrace Competition	131
22. Stay in the Moment	139
23. Strive to Be the Best: Locally, Nationally, and Globally	144
24. Building the Best TEAM	150
25. Handling Pressure Situations	161
26. Commitment and Mental Toughness	167
27. The Joy of the Journey	173
28. Giving Back	178
29. Building Your Brand: Modern Day Business-Minded Individuals	188
30. Relationship Building	197
31. Networking – Key Tasks for Building Success	204
32. Online Networking Platforms	213
33. Gratitude	220
34. Giving Oneself Selfless Success	226
35. Two Critical Life Decisions: Profession and Partner	235
36. Entrepreneurship	241
37. Resiliency	248
38. Risk Management	255
39. Reputation Matters	260
40. Building a Winning Culture	264

41. Derailments	268
42. Exceeding Expectations	273
43. Mastering Delegation	279
44. How to Identify What the Missing Pieces Are in Your Life, Business, or Team	284
45. Clear Vision	292
46. Time Management	296
47. The Pursuit of "Peace of Mind" Success in Life, Business, and Sports	302

Achieving "PEACE OF MIND" in

Life, Business and Sports

Business-Minded, Modern Day Individuals

By Mike Ross

Chapter 1

What is Peace of Mind in Life, Business and Sports?

"Life is not a spectator sport. If you're going to spend your whole life in the grandstand just watching what goes on, in my opinion you're wasting your life." - Jackie Robinson

Definition of Peace of Mind

Peace of mind is the serene state of inner calm and unwavering tranquility that emerges from the profound realization of one's purpose and achievements. It is the deep assurance that your journey, shaped by dedication, resilience, and tireless effort, has aligned with the path of true success—whether in life, business, or sports. This state transcends fleeting triumphs; it is the unshakable confidence that you not only belong at the pinnacle of excellence but also are fully prepared to thrive amidst its challenges. Achieving this harmony between preparation and accomplishment is a transformative milestone, marking a profound sense of fulfillment and inner mastery.

Peace of Mind in Life

In life, peace of mind is essential in various scenarios:

- **Achieving Personal Goals**: Whether getting a promotion, completing a personal project, or maintaining healthy relationships, knowing that you've put in your best effort and seeing the results from your efforts can bring a deep sense of satisfaction and calm.

- **Financial Stability**: Being financially secure can significantly contribute to peace of mind. Knowing that you have a safety net and are prepared for future expenses brings a sense of calm, relief and security.

- **Health and Well-Being**: Taking care of your physical and mental health is crucial. Regular exercise, balanced nutrition, and mindfulness can lead to a more peaceful mind.

- **Work-Life Balance**: Striking a healthy balance between your professional and personal life ensures that neither aspect will be neglected. This balance helps reduce stress and increase overall happiness and will achieve calm.

Peace of Mind in Business

- **Satisfied Customers**: Nothing will bring you more peace of mind than knowing your customers are well-taken care of during each stage of their relationship with you. Running a business can be a constant juggle. Making sure your stakeholders are satisfied will bring you more success and calmness in the long run.

- **Success**: Success isn't simply having a great business but being happy and living a life that makes you proud. Always remember to *celebrate your accomplishments* when you reach your goals with your employees and colleagues. Just can't sustain working 24/7 and have balance in your life. This is why celebrating your successes is part of a balanced lifestyle and peace of mind.

- **Health and Well-Being**: Taking care of your physical and mental health is crucial. Regular exercise, balanced nutrition, and mindfulness practices can lead to a more peaceful state of mind and longevity as a leader.

Peace of Mind in Sports

In the realm of sports, peace of mind plays a vital role in performance and overall well-being:

- **Preparation and Training**: Athletes often find peace of mind knowing they've trained and are well-prepared for their competition. This confidence can enhance their performance.

- **Focus and Concentration**: Mental calm allows athletes to focus better and perform under pressure. It helps them make quick decisions and maintain composure during critical moments.

- **Post-Performance Reflection**: After a game or competition, reflecting on your performance and knowing you gave it your best effort brings peace, regardless of the outcome. It's about enjoying the process and growth rather than just the result. Acknowledge the mistakes and put together a solution to solve future problems.

Achieving Peace of Mind is essential in business, life and sports. The pursuit of peace of mind is a *continuous journey*. How will you know you're on the right path? Keep working towards your goals, maintain balance, and cherish the moments of tranquility that come your way.

Peace of mind is achieved through excellent preparation, effort, and balance, leading to calm and satisfaction. By striving to do your best and enjoying the fruits of your labor, you can cultivate peace of mind in all areas of your life.

Peace of mind is not a destination, but a state achieved through preparation, effort, and balance. It arises when your actions align with your values, your hard work bears fruit, and you savor moments of stillness.

You're on the right path when your goals feel meaningful, your efforts purposeful, and you find calm in the present. It's not about perfection but about progress—living with intention, resilience, and gratitude. By nurturing this harmony, the journey itself becomes the reward, bringing peace to all areas of your life.

Chapter 2

If You Don't Ask, You Won't Get

"Ask for what you want and be prepared to get it!" — Maya Angelou

Renowned poet and activist Maya Angelou emphasizes the power of asking with confidence. Successful individuals understand that articulating their needs can open doors, prompting rewarding responses or negotiations.

"You miss 100% of the shots you don't take." — Wayne Gretzky

Wayne Gretzky, one of the greatest hockey players, underscores that inaction leads to missed opportunities. In the business world, failing to ask for what you need or want means forgoing potential successes and advancements.

The adage "If you don't ask, you won't get" holds profound truth in life, business, and sports. It's a simple yet powerful principle that transcends professional boundaries, impacting entrepreneurs, business professionals, athletes, parents, and coaches. This chapter explores how asking—whether for help, resources, or opportunities—can fundamentally change your trajectory and unlock doors that seemed permanently closed, empowering you to take control of your journey.

The Power of the Ask

Overcoming Shyness and Fear

It's natural to hesitate when asking for something, especially if you are shy or unsure. However, it's important to remember that the person you are contacting is unaware of your internal fear or hesitation. They only see your request. By overcoming this barrier, you open yourself to opportunities that might otherwise pass you by. Imagine the deals, partnerships, or guidance you might miss out on simply because you didn't ask.

Identifying the Givers

The world is full of individuals naturally inclined to give, support, and mentor. These people derive satisfaction from helping others achieve their goals, sharing their expertise, or simply being part of your mission. By asking, you allow these "givers" to fulfill their desire to contribute, creating a mutually beneficial relationship. Think about the business mentors who have shaped careers or the supportive coaches who have guided athletes to success—all because someone dared to ask.

Overcoming the Fear of Rejection

What is the worst that can happen, if you ask? The most common fear is getting a reply of "no." Remembering that a "no" is not the end of the road is essential. As my daughter Christine wisely says, "No means Next." Each "no" is an opportunity to move forward, reassess, and seek new paths toward your goals. Embracing this mindset transforms rejection from a personal setback into a stepping stone for growth and resilience. By understanding that a "no" doesn't define your worth or potential, you empower yourself to continue asking with confidence and determination.

Asking in Business

Negotiating the Deal

In business, negotiation is an art that often begins with a simple ask. Whether seeking a better price from a supplier or proposing a new venture to a potential partner, asking is the first essential step. You set the stage for dialogue and negotiation by articulating your needs and desires clearly. Remember, the worst response you can receive is a "no," but without asking, the answer is always "no."

Seeking Mentorship

Mentorship can be a game-changer for entrepreneurs and business professionals. However, mentorship doesn't just happen. It often requires reaching out, expressing admiration for someone's work, and asking for guidance. Many established professionals will share their knowledge and experience if approached respectfully. You gain insights and expand your network by asking, opening doors to new opportunities.

Asking in Sports

Requesting Feedback and Training

Athletes thrive on feedback. Asking coaches for specific feedback or additional training can significantly improve performance. Coaches appreciate athletes who are proactive about their development and eager to improve. By asking, athletes demonstrate their commitment and readiness to excel.

Securing Sponsorships

Sponsorships are crucial in an athlete's career, providing financial support and resources. However, securing sponsorships often requires athletes to seek them out actively. Reaching out to potential sponsors and articulating what you can offer increases your chances of securing valuable partnerships.

Asking in Life

Building Stronger Relationships

In personal relationships, asking for what you need, such as time, understanding, or support is vital for building strong connections. People aren't mind readers, and voicing your needs helps foster open communication and mutual respect.

Communication is the Key

The key to success is cultivating a relationship of trust, feeling safe, and mindfully communicating one's likes, dislikes, fears, and concerns.

Creating Opportunities

Life is full of opportunities waiting to be seized. Whether you're asking for a chance to lead a project at work or requesting help with a personal endeavor, taking the initiative to ask can lead to unexpected and rewarding experiences.

Achieving Peace of Mind: "If You Don't Ask, You Won't Get."

Finding peace of mind is about living authentically and being true to your needs and desires. If you don't ask for what you want or need—in life, business, and sports—you risk living with unmet expectations and silent frustrations.

In life, articulating your needs to friends and family can foster a more fulfilling and supportive environment. In business, seeking clarity and the resources necessary for success can lead to less stress and more confidence in your professional journey.

In sports, openly communicating your requirements, whether for better equipment or coaching, can significantly enhance your performance and satisfaction. Remember, unvoiced needs often remain unmet, whereas asking leads to possibilities and peace of mind. Don't shy away from the power of asking—embrace it and thrive in knowing that you've done your part to create the life you desire.

In every aspect of life, business, and sports, asking is a powerful tool that can lead to growth, success, and fulfillment. Courageously asking for what you need not only enhances your chances of achieving your goals but also enriches your relationships with those around you. Remember, many people are eager to help—you need to ask. This journey of asking and receiving is a path of growth and inspiration, motivating you to keep asking and keep growing.

Take the challenge today. What have you been hesitating to ask for? Please write it down, find the right person to ask, and take that step. You might be surprised at what you get.

Chapter 3

Overcoming Mistakes

"I've failed over and over and over again in my life and that is why I succeed." — Michael Jordan

Basketball legend Michael Jordan highlights that repeated failures teach valuable lessons, leading to success. By embracing mistakes and using them as learning experiences, individuals can develop strategies that contribute to their overall triumphs.

Everyone inevitably makes mistakes—it is a universal aspect of human experience with no exceptions. As we navigate the trials of growing up and mature through life's various stages, mistakes are a pivotal component of personal development.

The important distinction lies in avoiding critical errors, such as those that constitute criminal offenses, which can have lasting and severe consequences. Outside of these serious missteps, most mistakes are either fixable or fade from memory as time passes. This understanding allows individuals to approach errors with a mindset focused on learning and forgiveness, fostering a journey marked by continual growth and resilience.

Mistakes are an inevitable part of life, serving as valuable learning opportunities rather than setbacks. In life, embracing mistakes allows individuals to grow personally, fostering resilience and adaptability. In business, acknowledging and learning from errors can lead to innovation and improved strategies, ultimately driving success.

Likewise, mistakes on the field or court in sports push athletes to develop new techniques and refine their skills, often leading to breakthroughs and victories. Viewing mistakes through a positive lens encourages an environment where growth and improvement are always welcomed and celebrated; transforming challenges into stepping stones for future achievements.

Perspective plays a critical role in how we view our mistakes and their impact on our lives. Instead of dwelling on past errors, we can shift our perspective and focus on the lessons learned and opportunities for growth. It's essential to recognize that mistakes do not define us; how we handle them shapes who we are as individuals.

Changing Our Perspective: From Failure to Opportunity

Changing our perspective about mistakes requires a conscious effort to re-frame our thoughts. Instead of viewing failures as outcomes, we can see them as stepping stones towards success. By acknowledging what went wrong and learning from those experiences, we open ourselves to new possibilities and insights.

In a world filled with constant decisions and uncertainties, the power of perspective can be a guiding light. Whether you're a young adult stepping into adulthood, an entrepreneur navigating uncharted business territories, an athlete striving for excellence, a coach mentoring a team, a parent nurturing a child, or a managing partner leading an organization, perspective is a critical tool in shaping your life and the world around you.

1. Seek Diverse Perspectives

One of the most valuable actions you can take before making a significant decision is to gather insights from those around you. Friends, family, and professionals can offer different viewpoints you might not have considered. For instance, when making a career decision, you can seek advice from a mentor, a colleague, and a family member to get a well-rounded perspective.

- **Family and Friends**: These are people who know you well. They can provide personal insights that align with your values and long-term goals.

- **Professionals**: Experts in various fields can offer practical advice based on experience and knowledge you may not possess.

By incorporating diverse perspectives, you can create a broader foundation for your decisions.

2. Consider the Worst-Case Scenario

Often, we focus solely on the best possible outcomes, which can lead to unrealistic expectations and disappointment. It's crucial also to consider the worst-case scenario when making decisions.

- **Realism over Optimism**: While it's great to be optimistic, having a grounded perspective helps one prepare for potential setbacks and challenges.

- **Risk Assessment**: Understanding what could go wrong allows you to develop contingency plans and make more informed choices.

Acknowledging the worst-case scenario empowers you to make more balanced and strategic decisions.

3. List Positives and Negatives

Creating a list of pros and cons can clarify a decision and highlight factors you might not have initially considered.

- **Visual Clarity**: Writing everything down can help you visualize the impact and weight of each factor.

- **Objective Analysis** encourages objectivity, enabling one to see beyond emotional impulses and focus on logical reasoning.

A thoughtful evaluation of positives and negatives can simplify complex decisions and guide you toward the best path forward.

4. Eliminate Negativity

The people you surround yourself with profoundly influence your perspective and decisions. Removing harmful and toxic individuals from your inner circle can create a more positive environment and mindset, bringing a sense of relief and control. Also, don't spend years or a lifetime on someone who will not forgive you, especially after you sincerely apologize.

- **Influence and Energy**: Negative people can drain your energy and cloud your judgment, leading to poor decisions.

- **Supportive Environment**: A supportive network fosters growth, positivity, and resilience, allowing you to thrive and make better choices.

Clearing your life of Negativity paves the way for clarity, focus, and the power to shape your world positively.

5. Problem-Solving After a Mistake

Mistakes are often stepping stones to success, offering valuable lessons that can propel you forward. Instead of being disheartened by errors, view them as opportunities for growth and improvement, leading to a sense of accomplishment and confidence.

- **Identify the Issue**: Start by acknowledging what went wrong. This honest appraisal is essential to understanding the root cause of the mistake and preventing its recurrence.

- **Learn and Adapt**: Extract lessons from the experience and consider how you can adjust your strategies or approach. This adaptability is crucial for both personal and professional development.

- **Creative Solutions**: Employ problem-solving techniques like brainstorming or mind mapping to explore various solutions. For instance, if you've made a mistake in a project, you can use mind mapping to identify the root cause and brainstorm potential solutions. Innovative thinking can often lead to breakthroughs that might not have been apparent initially.

- **Resilience and Perseverance**: Accept that setbacks are part of any journey. Developing resilience helps you remain focused and motivated despite obstacles, ultimately allowing you to reach new levels of achievement.

6. Implement Change

Once the lessons from a mistake are identified, it is crucial to implement changes to ensure the mistake is not repeated. This might involve altering your workflow, setting clearer goals, or improving oral or written communication within a team. Effective implementation requires discipline and a commitment to personal growth.

- **Monitor Progress**: Regularly review your progress to ensure the changes have the desired effect. This could involve setting up checkpoints or seeking feedback from peers. Monitoring allows you to track improvements and make further adjustments if needed.

7. Forgiveness

Forgiveness is a powerful and essential element in maintaining healthy relationships and personal well-being. Once you sincerely apologize for a mistake, continuing to pursue forgiveness is necessary, but it is equally crucial to recognize when to let go. Spending years or a lifetime seeking absolution from someone who refuses to offer it can be emotionally draining and counterproductive. It is vital to assess whether your efforts are reciprocated, or the relationship has reached an impasse. Sometimes, moving on is the healthiest choice, allowing both parties to find peace and growth independently. Remember, valuing your self-forgiveness and acceptance is as important as obtaining it from others.

8. Stay Mindful

As you move forward, maintain awareness of past mistakes and their lessons. This mindfulness can help prevent complacency and keep you vigilant against similar pitfalls in the future. Remembering the cost of past errors can motivate continued diligence and improvement.

9. Therapy

Therapy can be an excellent alternative for individuals seeking additional support in navigating challenges and overcoming setbacks. Engaging with a professional therapist provides a safe space to explore personal issues, gain new perspectives, and develop tailored coping strategies. Whether dealing with past mistakes, stress, or personal development, therapy offers guidance in emotional regulation and self-discovery. Therapists can help identify underlying patterns and behaviors, facilitating meaningful change and growth. Embracing therapy as part of a holistic approach to personal, professional, and sports advancement can lead to a more resilient and adaptable mindset.

10. Athletes Making Mistakes - Moving Forward

For athletes, making mistakes is an inevitable part of the journey to reaching the next level of performance. Embracing these mistakes as learning opportunities is crucial in the development process. Mistakes teach valuable lessons about technique, decision-making, and resilience. By analyzing what went wrong and why, athletes can refine their skills and strategies, turning setbacks into stepping stones for future success. Moreover, the mental strength gained from overcoming adversity builds a robust mindset, which is essential for handling the pressures of high-level competition. Therefore, the ability to learn from mistakes and forge ahead with determination is a hallmark of successful athletes striving for excellence and getting to the next level ahead of a competitor with the same talent level as you!

Achieving Peace of Mind After Making a Mistake

Achieving peace of mind after making mistakes—whether in business, life, or sports—requires a thoughtful and compassionate approach. Begin by accepting the error for what it is: a part of your journey that contributes to growth rather than a measure of failure. Reflection is crucial, allowing you to understand the root of the mistake and what you can learn from it.

In business, this might involve analyzing decision-making processes and considering how to adjust strategies. It might mean focusing on personal improvement and resilience in life and sports. Practicing self-compassion is essential; recognize that everyone makes mistakes, and what matters most is how you respond and move forward. Cultivate a mindset of growth, where mistakes are viewed as valuable lessons.

Finally, engage in meditation or therapy to process emotions and restore inner calm. Doing so can transform mistakes into stepping stones towards a more mindful and enriched path.

By effectively addressing mistakes, you empower yourself to make informed decisions, build resilience, and continuously evolve on your path to success.

Chapter 4

Strategy: Outmaneuvering Any Rival

"It's not the will to win that matters—everyone has that. It's the will to prepare to win that matters." — Paul "Bear" Bryant

This powerful quote by football coach Paul Bear Bryant points to the necessity of preparation and strategy over mere desire. Success in sports is not just about wanting to win but preparing meticulously and strategically to outlast opponents.

Know the Rules

Understanding the rules - whether it's in life, business, sports, or any competitive arena—is crucial. This knowledge empowers you to exploit loopholes with your competition, avoid penalties, and use the system to your advantage, giving you a sense of control and confidence in your strategic decisions. Many successful entrepreneurs and athletes do not take the time to learn all the rules and laws, thus leading to crucial lapses, losses and disappointments.

Thinking Strategically

It would help if you thought strategically to gain the upper hand in any competitive environment. This means not just reacting to events as they happen but anticipating moves and countermoves and planning several steps ahead. Preparation is a crucial key to success and peace of mind in life, business and sports.

Target Audience

Entrepreneurs

For entrepreneurs, strategic thinking is essential for navigating the complexities of starting and growing a business. From identifying market opportunities to outsmarting competitors, knowing how to think strategically can be the difference between success and failure. Continued preparation and research which may forecast a down year for your business next year should mean to make some cuts anticipated the recession.

Business Executives

In the corporate world, executives face daily challenges that require quick yet strategic decision-making. This guide helps business leaders understand how to position their companies for long-term success, manage risks, and gain a competitive edge.

Competitive Athletes

Athletes can significantly benefit from strategic thinking. Beyond physical training, understanding the psychology of competition, studying opponents, and making split-second strategic decisions can elevate performance and lead to victory. Some positions in sports requiring a high IQ for success are the Quarterback in football, catcher in baseball and point guard in basketball. Today's new "Pay to Play" world in High School and College Sports opens up a new dynamic and requires business- minded male and female student-athletes.

Developing the right strategy for success in life, business, and sports involves several key steps. Here's a structured approach you can follow:

1. **Set Clear Goals**

    - **Life**: Define what success means to you personally. This could include relationships, health, and personal growth.

    - **Business**: Establish short-term and long-term objectives. Identify your mission and vision.

    - **Sports**: Set performance goals (e.g., improving your time, mastering a technique).

2. **Assess Your Current Situation**

    - Conduct a SWOT analysis (Strengths, Weaknesses, Opportunities, Threats) for each area.

    - Identify resources available to you, including time, finances, and support systems.

3. **Develop a Plan**

    - **Life**: Create a balanced life plan that includes work, leisure, and personal development.

    - **Business**: Develop a business strategy that includes marketing, operations, and financial management.

    - **Sports**: Outline a training regimen, including practice, nutrition, and recovery.

4. **Learn Continuously**

    - Stay informed about trends and best practices in your areas of interest.

    - Invest in education, whether through formal courses, workshops, or self-study.

5. Build a Support Network

- Surround yourself with mentors, peers, and professionals who can provide guidance and encouragement.
- Networking can open doors and provide new opportunities.

6. Stay Adaptable

- Be ready to adjust your strategy based on feedback and changing circumstances.
- Embrace failure as a learning opportunity rather than a setback.

7. Monitor Progress

- Regularly evaluate your progress against your goals.
- Use metrics to measure success in business and sports, and reflect on personal growth in life.

8. Maintain a Positive Mindset

- Cultivate resilience and a growth mindset.
- Practice mindfulness or other techniques to manage stress and maintain focus.

9. Take Action

- Break your plans into actionable steps and start implementing them.
- Consistent action is key to turning strategies into results.

10. Reflect and Iterate

- Periodically reflect on what's working and what isn't.
- Be willing to revise your strategy based on your experiences.

By following these steps and remaining committed to your vision, you can develop effective strategies for success in life, business, and sports.

Application Examples

Business Scenario

Example: An entrepreneur launching a new product must strategically plan the launch to outmaneuver competitors. This involves market research, timing the launch when competitors are weakest, and using marketing tactics to highlight their product's unique selling points.

Sports Scenario

Example: A baseball coach understands the rules so well that he designs offensive schemes to apply relentless pressure on the opponent's defense. This stress causes the defense to make critical – instantaneous decisions, often resulting in mistakes and runs scored by the offense.

Personal Development Scenario

Example: An individual aiming for a job promotion can use strategic thinking to identify key decision-makers, understand what they value most, and align their contributions to meet those needs, increasing their visibility and promotion chances.

Focus on Continuous Learning

Always seek knowledge and improvement. Staying informed about new developments in your field or industry will enable you to innovate and remain ahead of your competition. This commitment to learning is not just a strategy, it's a mindset that will inspire and guide your personal development journey. Implementing these tips will equip you with the tools to outsmart and outperform your rivals across various life, business, and sports domains.

Strategy: It's Your Blueprint for Success

Whether you're an entrepreneur looking to disrupt an industry, a business executive aiming to steer your company to new heights, or a competitive athlete seeking to win the ultimate championship: **unlock your strategic potential.** Get started today and see how far strategic thinking can take you! With the right strategy, success is not just a possibility, it's a probability.

Chapter 5

The Art of "Negotiating"

"You can't always get what you want. But if you try sometimes, you just might find, you get what you need." — **The Rolling Stones**

The wisdom in this lyric suggests that while achieving every goal in negotiation isn't possible, persistence and adaptability can yield favorable and sometimes unexpected outcomes.

Negotiation is a vital skill that transcends various aspects of life, including personal relationships, business dealings, and competitive sports. Effective negotiation can lead to better understanding and cooperation among family members and friends, enabling individuals to resolve conflicts and achieve mutual satisfaction.

I've found success in negotiations by asking the other party two key questions:

1. **How?** How can we resolve this issue?

2. **What?** What steps can we take to solve this problem?

Allow them time to respond to these questions. Often, their answers will align with what you're seeking. At that point, you can move toward closing the deal. Remember to **listen** carefully to their responses.

Successful negotiations often determine the terms of partnerships, contracts, and pricing in the business world, directly impacting a company's growth and profitability.

Similarly, athletes and coaches must negotiate strategies, contracts, and team dynamics to ensure optimal performance and success. Modern day athletes in high school and college are facing financial decisions as teenagers which may require negotiable scenarios with college collectives and brands for lucrative deals. Thus, these talented athletes are ushering in a new wave of entrepreneurs in the world. Mastering negotiation techniques not only empowers individuals to navigate challenges but also instills a sense of capability and control, enabling them to achieve their goals across these domains.

Developing the Basic Negotiating Skills

1. **Preparation:**

    - Research and understand the needs and motivations of both parties.

    - Know your goals and what items you are willing to compromise on.

2. **Active Listening:**

    - Listen more than you speak. This helps to build rapport and understand the other party's perspective.

3. **Clear Communication:**

    - Be articulate and clear about what your needs and expectations are.

    - Avoid jargon that might confuse the other party.

In Life

- **Emotional Intelligence:**

    - Recognize and manage your emotions and those of others. This can help de-escalate tense situations.

- **Win-Win Solutions**:
    - Aim for outcomes that satisfy both parties. This fosters long-term relationships.

In Business

- **Building Relationships**:
    - Establish trust and rapport with others before entering negotiations. This practice can lead to more favorable outcomes.
- **Leverage**:
    - Understand your value and use it to your advantage. Know when to walk away if terms are unfavorable.

In Sports

- **Team Collaboration**:
    - Negotiate roles and responsibilities within a team. Open communication can enhance teamwork and performance.
- **Game Strategy**:
    - Negotiate tactics with your coach and teammates, ensuring everyone is aligned on goals and strategies.

Communication and Listening

In addition to practical skills like negotiation, *effective communication* is crucial for fostering collaboration and understanding. It involves not only the ability to convey information clearly but also to listen actively and empathetically. Good communicators can adapt their messages to suit their audience, utilizing various channels and methods to ensure engagement. Whether it's through written correspondence, verbal discussions, or digital platforms, strong communication skills play a pivotal role in resolving misunderstandings, thereby building relationships and facilitating teamwork. By prioritizing open dialogue, individuals and organizations can cultivate a culture of trust and respect, leading to enhanced creativity and problem-solving.

Building Your "Team" Culture in Sports and Business for Better Negotiation Results

Build your team with individuals who love the game and are selfless. This will require at times to not hire or fire very talented individuals. However, in the long run, all decisions made in the company or team will be based on these two traits making negotiations for salaries much easier and less stressful to avoid moral and bring the organization down.

Application and Results: Not Always What You Were Hoping For

Sometimes, negotiations result in outcomes where both sides may not feel entirely satisfied, yet these compromises are essential for progress. In many scenarios, the parties involved have differing priorities, interests, and expectations, which can lead to a stalemate or dissatisfaction with the final agreement. However, reaching a consensus—even if it doesn't meet all desires—can pave the way for future cooperation and growth. By acknowledging and accepting the necessity of these compromises, individuals and organizations can move forward, maintain relationships, and create opportunities for more harmonious dealings in the future. This understanding and acceptance of compromises foster a collaborative environment that ultimately benefits all parties involved.

Establish Your Boundaries of Best and Worst-Case Scenarios

When setting boundaries in negotiations, it's crucial to establish both the best and worst-case scenarios to guide your approach. The best-case scenario involves achieving your ideal outcome, whether the most favorable terms in a contract or a resolution that perfectly aligns with your objectives. Clearly defining this boundary lets you focus on your desired goals and objectives throughout the negotiation process. Conversely, the worst-case scenario represents the minimum acceptable outcome you will accept, which could involve settling for less-than-ideal terms but still ensuring that your basic needs and interests have been met. By understanding your limits, you can avoid making concessions jeopardizing your overall position. Establishing these boundaries fosters confidence, enabling you to negotiate more effectively and make informed decisions based on the evolving dynamics of discussions.

Achieving Successful Negotiations in Life, Business, and Sports

Successful negotiations in life, business, and sports hinge on knowing the rules, preparation, adaptability, listening, and effective communication. By establishing clear boundaries and understanding your ideal outcomes and acceptable compromises, you can navigate negotiations confidently and clearly. Ultimately, the ability to negotiate effectively can lead to enhanced personal relationships, fruitful business partnerships, and cohesive team performance in sports, underscoring the importance of negotiation as a vital life skill. Remember, most times in the negotiating process, both parties will be disappointed in the outcome. The key is to sacrifice a little to move on in your life's journey and chalk this up for a learning experience.

Chapter 6

Integrity Across All Realms

"In looking for people to hire, you look for three qualities: integrity, intelligence, and energy. And if they don't have the first, the other two will kill you." — **Warren Buffett**

Integrity is a fundamental value that transcends various aspects of life, including our personal lives, business practices, and sports. Whether you're a leader, athlete, parent, or business owner, integrity is a guiding principle that shapes your actions and decisions. This chapter explores the importance of integrity in these three realms and highlights the interconnections of ethics, elite performance, well-being, and sportsmanship.

Integrity in Life

Integrity in life involves being honest, fair, and consistent. It's about doing the right thing, even when no one is watching. For parents, this means being role models for their children and teaching them the values of honesty, respect, and responsibility.

Key Points:

- **Role Models:** As parents, you are the first role models for your children. Your everyday actions, demonstrating integrity, play a crucial role in instilling these values in the next generation.

- **Consistency:** Living with integrity means being consistent in your values and actions building trust and respect among family, friends, and community members.

Example:

- **Example of Integrity:** A parent who returns extra change given by mistake at a store demonstrates honesty and sets a positive example for their children.

- **Example of Lack of Integrity:** A parent who cheats on a partner breaks trust and sets a negative example for their children.

Integrity in Business

Business integrity is **conducting business practices by following a moral and ethical framework**. As with personal integrity, business integrity requires honesty and consistency and holds one accountable for one's actions, even when nobody's watching.

Integrity in business is crucial for building a reputation, gaining customer trust, and ensuring long-term success. Business owners and leaders expect to uphold ethical standards, treat employees fairly, and operate transparently.

Key Points:

- **Ethical Standards:** Businesses that prioritize and uphold ethical practices will earn the trust of employees, underscoring the weight of your decisions as a business owner.

- **Transparency:** Being open and honest about business practices and decisions helps build a culture of integrity within the organization.

- **Leadership:** Leaders who demonstrate integrity inspire their teams to act honestly and accountable.

Example:

- **Example of Integrity:** A business owner who acknowledges a mistake in a product and offers a transparent solution to customers demonstrates integrity.

- **Example of Lack of Integrity:** A business that falsely advertises its products to boost sales damages its reputation and customer trust.

Integrity in Sports

Integrity in sports encompasses fair play, respect for opponents, and adherence to rules. Athletes are often seen as role models, and their actions can influence fans, especially young aspiring athletes.

Key Points:

- **Sportsmanship:** True sportsmanship involves respecting opponents, officials, and the game, regardless of the outcome.

- **Fair Play:** Competing honestly and within the rules is essential for maintaining the integrity of sports.

- **Role Models:** Athletes who demonstrate integrity inspire others to engage in sports with the same values.

Example:

- **Example of Integrity:** An athlete who admits to a foul, even if the referee missed it, exemplifies true sportsmanship.

- **Example of Lack of Integrity:** Doping in sports represents a significant breach of integrity, undermining the fairness and spirit of competition.

THE FOUR-WAY-TEST is the crucial base on all decisions made in life... What does it mean? This is one of the best guidelines to integrity in all aspects of life, business and sports

The Rotary International Four-Way Test is the cornerstone of all action. It has been for years, and it will be in the future.

All the things we think, say, or do:

1. Is it the TRUTH?

2. Is it FAIR to all concerned?

3. Will it build GOODWILL and BETTER FRIENDSHIPS?

4. Will it be BENEFICIAL to all concerned?

Achieving Peace of Mind with Integrity

Achieving peace of mind is intrinsically linked to the practice of integrity. When individuals uphold their values and act consistently with their principles, they cultivate a sense of inner calm and confidence. This alignment between beliefs and actions reduces guilt and anxiety, as decisions made with ethical consideration foster a trusting environment.

Being *truthful and accountable* in personal life encourages healthy relationships, while integrity builds credibility and long-term partnerships in business.

For athletes, maintaining integrity garners respect from peers and competitors and reinforces their self-respect, ultimately contributing to mental clarity and focus.

By embracing integrity as a foundational pillar in all areas, individuals can confidently navigate life's complexities, thereby achieving lasting peace of mind.

Chapter 7

Goal Setting

"Don't follow the trends. Set your own goals and achieve them." — **Mark Cuban**

This quote by Mark Cuban encourages individuals to focus on personal ambition and goal setting, rather than getting swept up in external trends. It underlines the importance of defining one's own success parameters and pursuing them with determination.

"It's not about money or connections — it's the willingness to set goals and outwork / outlearn everyone." — **Mark Cuban**

This quote emphasizes that setting and achieving goals relies more on effort and the commitment to continuous learning than on existing wealth or relationships. Cuban's words inspire individuals to rely on their work ethic and dedication to reach their goals, regardless of their starting point.

Goal Setting Success Stories

Example 1: **Personal Life**

- **Goal**: "I want to gain 15 lbs. of muscle in 6 months."

- **Outcome**: Lino set a specific muscle gain goal with a clear timeline. He followed a structured diet and exercise plan, tracked his progress weekly, and successfully gained the weight. Lino celebrated by hosting a healthy dinner party with friends and family.

Example 2: **School**

- **Goal**: "I want to achieve an A in my math class this semester."

- **Outcome**: John set his sights on earning an A in math. He created a study schedule, attended extra tutoring sessions, and consistently reviewed his notes. His hard work paid off, and he celebrated his achievement by sharing the news with his family and treating himself to a new book.

Example 3: **Sports**

- **Goal**: "I want to score ten goals this soccer season."

- **Outcome**: Sarah aims to score ten (10) goals during her soccer season. She practices shooting techniques daily, analyzes her game performance, and works closely with her coach. By the season's end, Sarah had reached and exceeded her goal. She celebrates by treating her teammates to a pizza party.

Example 4: **Business**

- **Goal**: "Christine wants to sell $450,000 per month for my company for 12 months, totaling $5,400,000 in sales."

- **Outcome**: Christine worked hard on networking, marketing, and establishing relationships with power partners in her business network. Christine also took webinars on sales and closing deals. Shattering her yearly sales goal by $1,250,00, she celebrated by taking her work staff out to dinner and going on a much-deserved vacation.

Celebrate Your Achievements

This you absolutely MUST do. Achieving your goals is a significant accomplishment, and it's *essential* to celebrate your successes.

Whether you share your achievement with family, business partner, teammates or friends, reward yourself with a gift, treat, dinner or trip - acknowledging your hard work and dedication is a form of self-appreciation and recognition that boosts motivation and morale.

Additional Tips for Achieving Your Goals

1. Please write down your goals: This helps to solidify them and serves as a visual reminder to keep you motivated.

2. Break down larger goals into smaller ones: Sometimes, big goals can seem overwhelming, so breaking them into smaller achievable steps can make them more manageable.

3. Track your progress regularly. Set checkpoints along the way to evaluate your progress and adjust your approach if necessary.

4. Stay focused and positive: It's normal to face challenges or setbacks while pursuing your goals, but stay focused even if you come up a little short; it is still an improvement.

Achieving Peace of Mind Through Goal Setting

Goal setting is a powerful tool in pursuing peace of mind, providing individuals with a clear direction and purpose. People can transform their aspirations into actionable plans by establishing specific, measurable, achievable, relevant, and time-bound (SMART) goals. This process enhances focus and motivation and reduces feelings of overwhelm, as breaking larger objectives into manageable steps makes them more attainable. Furthermore, setting goals fosters a sense of ownership and accountability, which can significantly diminish self-doubt and anxiety. As individuals achieve their milestones, they experience a boost in self-efficacy, reinforcing their belief in their capabilities and promoting a positive mindset.

Chapter 8

The Five Choices in Everything We Do

This chapter was a favorite of the University of Alabama football coach, **Nick Saban**. Everyone has five fundamental choices regarding success in every aspect of life, business, and sports. Here's a breakdown of Coach Saban's choices and their impacts:

1. Choose to be Bad

Choosing to be wrong means you don't care and put forth no effort. This choice might be the easiest, but it comes with significant consequences:

- **Lack of Growth**: You won't develop new skills or improve existing ones.

- **Missed Opportunities**: Doors that could have opened remain closed.

- **Negative Impact**: Your attitude and performance can drag down teams, projects, and personal relationships.

2. Choose to be Average

Choosing to be average means you do just enough to get by. While this might seem like a safe choice, it limits your potential:

- **Minimal Progress**: Growth is stagnant, and you only meet the bare minimum expectations.

- **Limited Recognition**: You blend in with the crowd and rarely stand out.

- **Missed Potential**: You need to tap into what you can achieve.

3. Choose to be Good

Being good involves a decent amount of effort and care. It means you are reliable and competent:

- **Steady Growth**: Consistently strive for improvement and skill development.

- **Positive Recognition**: People notice your effort and value your contributions.

- **Foundation for Excellence**: This level sets the stage for achieving higher levels of success.

4. Choose to be Excellent

Excellence requires a solid commitment to high standards in all you do. It involves:

- **Excellent Work Ethic**: A solid dedication to consistently putting in the effort.

- **Desire to Excel**: An intrinsic motivation to be among the best.

- **Persistence**: Continuously pushing forward despite obstacles.

- **Resiliency**: Bouncing back from failures and learning from them.

- **Dedication**: A long-term commitment to maintaining and exceeding high standards.

Impact of Choosing Excellence

- **High Achievement**: Remarkable accomplishments in your field.

- **Respect and Recognition**: You are a leader and expert in your field.

- **Personal Fulfillment**: Satisfaction from knowing you gave your best.

5. Choose to be Elite

Choosing to be elite means striving to be at your absolute best. This choice demands the highest level of commitment and embodies all qualities of excellence but taken to the next level:

- **Special Work Ethic**: Relentless effort day in and day out.

- **Special Intense Desire** to be at the top.

- **Special Unyielding Persistence** in the face of significant challenges.

- **Special Extraordinary Resiliency** to overcome repeated failures and setbacks.

- **Special Total Dedication** to your craft, often at the expense of other pursuits.

Impact of Choosing to be Elite

- **Top of Your Field**: You become a benchmark for others.

- **Legacy**: You leave a lasting impact on your industry or sport.

- **Ultimate Fulfillment**: Achieving your ultimate potential.

Achieving Peace of Mind by Striving to be Elite in Life, Business, and Sports

Striving to be elite in life, business, and sports offers a profound pathway to achieving peace of mind. Setting high standards encourages individuals to push their boundaries and unlock their full potential, fostering a sense of achievement and self-worth. In business, aspiring to be elite cultivates a business mindset of continuous improvement and innovation, ultimately leading to greater satisfaction and fulfillment from one's work.

Similarly, in sports, the pursuit of elite performance drives athletes to commit to rigorous training and discipline, instilling a strong sense of purpose and resilience. This relentless pursuit enhances skills and fosters a positive mindset as individuals learn to navigate challenges and celebrate progress. By embracing this commitment to eliteness across all areas of life, individuals not only enrich their experiences but also find more profound peace of mind in the knowledge that they are pursuing their best selves.

I encourage you to reflect on these choices and consider how you can apply them in your own life, business, or sports endeavors.

Chapter 9

Starting is Very Important...Finishing is Crucial!

Usain Bolt has said many famous things, including, **"Worrying gets you nowhere,"** and **"Don't think about the start of the race, think about the ending."**

"The way to get started is to quit talking and begin doing." — Walt Disney

Walt Disney, the founder of The Walt Disney Company, encourages entrepreneurs to take action rather than just contemplate ideas, highlighting the importance of initiative and execution in achieving finally business success.

A strong start sets the stage, igniting our ambitions with the spark of possibility. Ultimately, the measure of success lies not in the momentum of our beginnings but in our ability to cross the finish line. Finishing what we start embodies our commitment to seeing our dreams transform into achievements. It's about overcoming the mid-journey fatigue, the unexpected obstacles, and the tempting diversions. Each step taken towards completing our goals fortifies our character and amplifies our potential.

Development of Discipline and Consistency

Training for a marathon demands a disciplined schedule—regular long runs, strength training, and recovery periods. Adhering to this strict regimen instills a habit of consistency. The discipline learned here can translate into other areas of life, such as work ethic and personal relationships.

Enhanced Problem-Solving Skills

During training, a runner might face various obstacles, such as injuries or scheduling conflicts. Finding ways to overcome these issues through medical advice, adjusting routines, or finding balance with other life commitments enhances problem-solving skills.

Boost in Confidence

Crossing the finish line after months of hard training is an immense confidence booster. Achieving such a formidable goal proves that it is possible to tackle and conquer even the most intimidating challenges with the right effort and perseverance.

Understanding the Value of Incremental Progress

Marathon training is a prime example of how small, daily efforts accumulate into significant achievements. This understanding helps in setting and achieving long-term goals in other complex or lengthy projects in personal or professional life.

Business

Consider the story of Sarah, a young graphic designer who faced significant challenges in her career when tasked with leading a major project for her company. The project involved creating a complete branding package for a high-profile client, including a new logo, website design, and multiple marketing materials. This is Sarah's first time leading such a significant initiative, especially with a tight deadline and high expectations.

Challenge and Initial Doubt

Initially, Sarah was overwhelmed. The scope of the project was far beyond what she had managed before. She doubted her ability to meet the client's expectations and lead her team effectively. The fear of failure loomed large.

Taking the Leap

Despite her fears, Sarah committed to the project. She organized her team, delegated tasks according to each member's strengths, and scheduled regular meetings for progress updates and brainstorming sessions. She also sought advice from more experienced colleagues when necessary, showing a willingness to learn and adapt.

Overcoming Obstacles

The project was fraught with challenges, including differing opinions within the team and technical issues with the website launch. Sarah had to mediate conflicts and find solutions under pressure, which pushed her out of her comfort zone and required her to take quick, decisive action.

Successful Completion and Client Approval

After weeks of hard work, late nights, and continuous refinements, we completed the project to the client's satisfaction. The client praised the innovative approach and the quality of the work, explicitly highlighting the leadership that made it all possible.

Boost in Confidence

Completing this project had a profound impact on Sarah. It significantly boosted her confidence, proving to herself that she could handle the pressure of big projects and lead a team effectively. This experience was a turning point in her career, leading to more responsibilities and a promotion.

Broader Impact

The success of the project not only elevated Sarah's self-esteem but also earned her respect and recognition within her professional community. She became more vocal in meetings, proactive in proposing new ideas, and willing to take on challenging tasks.

Sarah's story illustrates how stepping up to a difficult task, despite initial doubts, and seeing it through to completion can significantly boost an individual's confidence. This newfound confidence can transform their professional trajectory and open up new opportunities for growth and leadership.

Sports

Marathon Training is Not Just About Physical Endurance, but Also Building Emotional Resilience.

Throughout the training and the race, there are moments of doubt, pain, and the urge to give up. Overcoming these mental challenges builds emotional resilience, which is a valuable asset when facing future life stresses and adversities. Completing a challenging task, like running a marathon, can be a transformative experience. For someone new to long-distance running, the goal of finishing a marathon is a formidable physical and mental challenge. The journey involves consistent training, dietary adjustments, and the development of endurance and resilience. The process of overcoming these hurdles leads to significant personal growth in several ways.

Achieving Peace of Mind When Starting is Important, but Finishing is Crucial!

Starting new projects or endeavors generates excitement and motivation. However, the true essence of *peace of mind is completing these tasks*. The journey from beginning to end can be fraught with challenges and uncertainties that test our resolve.

Yet, it's this very journey that prepares us for the future. In both personal and professional realms, this commitment to seeing things through fosters resilience and enables individuals to approach future challenges with increased confidence and a deeper understanding of their capabilities.

The world awaits your brilliance—shine brightly, relentlessly, and triumphantly!

Chapter 10

Leadership...the Essence of Effectiveness

"If your actions inspire others to dream more, learn more, do more and become more, you are a leader." — **John Quincy Adams**

Former U.S. President John Quincy Adams illustrates that true leadership and success are determined by one's ability to empower and uplift others towards greater personal and professional growth.

Let's Start Out with Examples of Ineffective Leadership:

1. **Indecisiveness**: When a leader is confronted with an important decision and they analyze repeatedly, delaying action. Don't waste everyone's time.

2. **Problem Solving Inability**: The key to getting to the next level. If you can't do this quickly or at all the family, company or team is doomed for failure.

3. **No Clarity with Priorities:** The leader issues 10-20 tasks and says ALL of these are important!

4. **The Leader Speaks in Technical Language Instead of Inspiring:** He leaves them bored and no clear path.

5. **Constantly Criticizing and No Positive Reinforcement:** One single mistake by an individual should not haunt them forever. Give the individual a chance to learn from their mistake.

6. **Never Communicating a Clear Vision:** Therefore, the team is left with no clarity for a path to success.

7. **Confine yourself to an office all day** instead of getting out in the hallways, job sites or on the field with the team.

8. **Exercising "power" is not true leadership:** True leadership is when individual's follow when they would otherwise have the freedom to *not* follow.

A hallmark of a great leader is understanding the importance of recognizing and utilizing the right talents effectively aligning people's strengths with the right roles. Here are a few key points on this topic:

1. **Identifying Strengths**: Effective leaders assess the unique skills and talents of their team members through evaluations, feedback, and open conversations.

2. **Strategic Placement**: By placing individuals in roles that match their skills, leaders can enhance productivity and job satisfaction. This involves understanding both the needs of the organization and the aspirations of the team.

3. **Fostering Development**: Great leaders also invest in their team's growth. This might include training, mentorship, or opportunities for skill enhancement, ensuring that team members can thrive in their positions.

4. **Creating a Collaborative Environment**: A successful leader builds a culture where team members can collaborate and leverage each other's skills, creating a more dynamic and effective team.

5. **Continuous Feedback**: Regular check-ins and feedback loops help leaders adjust roles and responsibilities as needed, ensuring that the team remains aligned and motivated.

Leadership is a transformative force that transcends titles and positions. True leaders inspire and motivate others towards a common goal. They have the unique ability to see beyond the present, envisioning future possibilities that others might not yet perceive. They are the architects of change, the catalysts who stimulate progress through innovation and strategic thinking.

Core Qualities of Effective Leaders

1. **Listening:** Listening is a vital part of being a great leader, as it can build trust, respect, and understanding with team members, family, and teammates. Leaders gain insight into their teams' needs and develop shared growth goals by listening.

2. **Conviction:** The team must feel your passion and your vision serves as a guiding star, not just for themselves but for everyone involved in the endeavor.

3. **Role Model: You Have Heard the Saying "Practice What You Preach."** Act on your core values and beliefs as the leader.

4. **Integrity and Authenticity:** Trust is foundational in Leadership. Leaders who act with integrity and authenticity inspire loyalty and respect from their teams. They are consistent, reliable, and uphold moral and ethical standards, making decisions that align with organizational values and societal norms.

5. **Resilience and Adaptability:** The path of Leadership is not just fraught with challenges, but defined by them. Influential leaders are not just resilient, but able to withstand setbacks without losing momentum. Moreover, they are not just adaptable, but capable of pivoting strategies in response to changing circumstances without sacrificing their core objectives.

6. **Communication Skills:** A leader must not just be an excellent communicator, but a masterful one who can convey complex

ideas clearly and persuasively. They must also be adept listeners, open to feedback, and able to engage in meaningful dialogues that encourage diverse viewpoints.

Becoming a leader in life, business, and sports involves a combination of personal development, skills acquisition, and practical experience. Here are some guiding principles:

1. **Self-Awareness**

- Understand your strengths and weaknesses.
- Reflect on your values and what drives you.

2. **Continuous Learning**

- Read books on leadership and personal development.
- Attend workshops, seminars, and training sessions.

3. **Set Clear Goals**

- Define your short-term and long-term goals.
- Create actionable plans to achieve them.

4. **Build Strong Relationships**

- Network with mentors and peers.
- Foster teamwork and collaboration.

5. **Develop Communication Skills**

- Practice active listening.
- Learn to articulate your thoughts clearly and persuasively.

6. **Lead by Example**
   - Demonstrate integrity and ethical behavior.
   - Show commitment and dedication in all your endeavors.

7. **Embrace Challenges**
   - Take calculated risks and learn from failures.
   - Stay resilient in the face of adversity.

8. **Inspire and Motivate Others**
   - Encourage and support team members.
   - Share your vision and get others excited about it.

9. **Adaptability**
   - Be open to change and new ideas.
   - Stay informed about trends in your field.

10. **Seek Feedback and Reflect**
    - Regularly ask for feedback from peers and mentors.
    - Reflect on your experiences and incorporate lessons learned.

11. **Best Leaders are "Hands On"**
    - Always put your personal touch on the company
    - Absolutely no excuse to be a detached / distant leader
    - But absolutely do not "Micro Manage"

11. **Be Accessible**
    - Open door to all input from team members

- Absolutely no excuse to be a detached / distant leader

In Sports

- **Practice Regularly:** Commitment to training and improvement is crucial.
- **Understand the Game:** Study strategies and develop tactical awareness.
- **Team Spirit:** Support and uplift your teammates.

In Business

- **Understand Your Industry:** Stay informed about market trends.
- **Innovate:** Be open to new ideas and processes.
- **Customer Focus:** Prioritize customer needs and feedback.

One of the toughest decisions a CEO, Coach or Entrepreneur will make is "Should I fire an employee or spend the time and resources to develop an employee who is not hitting the goals you projected".

Here Are Some Questions to Ask Yourself About Your Managers for You to Gain More Clarity:

1. How would you feel if they quit? Would you fight to get them back?
2. Would you consider a different position within the company they may be better suited for?
3. Do they have the WILL to continue?
4. Do they have the skills to continue?
5. Do they lack the core values of your company?

6. Are you losing other key people by keeping this person on your team (Is this person a "cancer")

7. Attract self-disciplined and self-motivated individuals who believe in your mission-never try to motivate the wrong individuals.

Bad to Elite Leadership Levels:

1. No Expertise

2. Expertise Developed

3. Teamwork Expertise learned

4. Management Expertise

5. Leadership Expertise

6. Elite leadership is a culmination of Level 1 through Level 5

Achieving Peace of Mind Through Leadership in Life, Business, and Sports

The defining hallmark of the most exceptional leaders lies in their ability to elevate everyone around them, unlocking potential and inspiring greatness in others.

This "elevation" manifests in tangible results through a variety of impactful ways:

1. **Enhanced Team Performance**: Leaders who uplift others cultivate a culture of collaboration and empowerment, leading to increased productivity, innovation, and the achievement of collective goals.

2. **Individual Growth**: By mentoring, coaching, and creating opportunities, these leaders help individuals hone their skills, build confidence, and reach new levels of personal and professional success.

3. **Stronger Relationships**: Their ability to foster trust, respect, and open communication strengthens connections within the team, resulting in greater cohesion and morale.

4. **Organizational Impact**: Elevating others creates a ripple effect, where empowered individuals contribute to a high-performing, adaptable, and resilient organization.

5. **Sustainable Success**: By prioritizing the development of others, these leaders build a legacy of capable, inspired individuals who carry forward their vision and values, ensuring long-term success.

In essence, this elevation translates into a thriving ecosystem where people and results flourish together.

Chapter 11

Mentorship

"The delicate balance of mentoring someone is not creating them in your own image, but giving them the opportunity to create themselves." — Steven Spielberg

Steven Spielberg echoes the transformative power and profound value of mentorship in shaping lives and fostering growth.

Introduction

Mentorship is the compass that guides individuals through the uncharted terrains of life, business, and sports. Whether you are an entrepreneur trying to launch a startup, a student navigating academic challenges or an athlete striving for excellence, the right mentor can be pivotal in helping you achieve your goals. This chapter explores the role of mentorship, the benefits it brings, and strategies to cultivate meaningful mentor-mentee relationships.

The Role of Mentorship

Mentorship is more than just guidance; it's a relationship that fosters growth, confidence, and resilience. A mentor is someone who provides wisdom, support, and encouragements, helping you unlock your potential while avoiding common pitfalls. They offer a unique blend of experience and insight that textbooks, courses, or seminars can never provide.

In Life

Life is an unpredictable journey, fraught with decisions that can profoundly impact our future. Mentors offer perspective. Whether it's a parent guiding a child, a teacher influencing a student, or a community leader inspiring the next generation. They provide the necessary scaffolding that helps individuals build their lives with purpose and direction.

In Business

The business landscape is a dynamic arena where competition is fierce, and innovation is key. Entrepreneurs who have mentors are more likely to succeed, as mentors can impart crucial knowledge about industry trends, business strategies, and networking. They serve as sounding boards for ideas, helping refine them into actionable plans. Mentors can also introduce entrepreneurs to their networks, opening doors that would otherwise remain closed.

In Sports

In sports, mentorship is vital for developing both physical and mental skills. Coaches play a critical role in honing athletic talent, but mentorship extends beyond technical training. It involves building character, instilling discipline, and fostering a winning mindset. Athletes with mentors learn to manage pressure, setbacks, and victories, emerging as well-rounded individuals on and off the field.

Benefits of Mentorship

1. **Accelerated Learning**: Mentorship provides access to a wealth of knowledge accumulated over years of experience, allowing mentees to learn faster and more effectively.

2. **Networking Opportunities**: Mentors can connect you with influential people and resources, broadening your professional and personal horizons.

3. **Personal Growth**: A mentor-mentee relationship encourages self-reflection and personal development, helping you become

more self-aware and confident.

4. **Support System**: Having a mentor means having someone who believes in your potential, motivating you during tough times and celebrating your successes.

Cultivating Meaningful Mentor-Mentee Relationships

Finding the right mentor requires effort, but the rewards are worth it. Here's how you can cultivate a successful mentorship relationship:

1. Identify Your Needs

Before seeking a mentor, clarify what you hope to achieve. Are you looking for career advice, personal growth, or specific skills? Understanding your needs will help you find a mentor whose expertise aligns with your goals.

2. Seek Compatibility

A strong mentor-mentee relationship is built on compatibility. Look for someone who shares your values and interests, and who you feel comfortable communicating with. Mutual respect and trust are essential components of a productive mentorship.

3. Be Proactive

Approach potential mentors with a clear proposition of what you seek and what you can offer in return. Be open-minded and willing to learn, showing genuine interest and appreciation for their time and insights.

4. Set Clear Goals

Establish clear objectives and expectations for the mentorship. Regularly review these goals to ensure progress and to maintain alignment between both parties.

5. Maintain Communication

Effective communication is the backbone of any successful mentorship. Schedule regular check-ins, provide updates on your progress, and be open to feedback. Remember, this is a two-way street—actively listen and contribute to the conversation.

Achieving Peace of Mind in Mentorship in Life, Business, and Sports

Mentorship is a powerful tool that can transform lives, shape careers, and build champions. Whether you're an entrepreneur striving to disrupt an industry, a student eager to excel, or an athlete aiming for gold, the guidance of a mentor can be invaluable.

Take the initiative to find and nurture these relationships and experience the profound impact of mentorship on your own personal and professional journeys.

"The people closest to me determine my level of success or failure. The better they are, the better I am. And if I want to go to the highest level, I can do it only with the help of other people. We have to take each other higher," attributed to John Wooden, a legendary basketball coach known for his emphasis on character development.

Chapter 12

The Power of Perseverance

This chapter delves into the transformative power of perseverance, exploring why it is a fundamental attribute in the quest for personal, professional, and athletic accomplishment. It shows how perseverance can turn challenges into stepping stones towards greatness, binding the fabric of success with resilience and relentless determination.

Understanding Perseverance

Perseverance is not just a passive continuation, but an active, steadfast pursuit of goals, regardless of obstacles. It is the **sustained effort** necessary to do something despite difficulties or delays in achieving success. Perseverance is what separates fleeting endeavors from fulfilled dreams.

Perseverance is a quality that has defined many of the world's most influential figures, each of whom faced immense challenges yet remained steadfast in their pursuits.

Here are a few notable examples:

1. Marie Curie

Background: Marie Curie was a physicist and chemist who conducted pioneering research on radioactivity.

Exemplification of Perseverance: Curie faced immense obstacles in her career due to her gender. Despite being often overlooked and undervalued by her male peers, she continued her research without faltering. She was the first woman to win a Nobel Prize and remains the only person to win in two different scientific fields.

Impact on Others: Curie's persistence in adversity opened doors for women in science, breaking gender barriers and setting a precedent for future generations. Her discoveries have had profound implications in science and medicine, inspiring countless individuals to pursue careers in these fields.

2. Abraham Lincoln

Background: Abraham Lincoln was the 16th President of the United States, leading the nation during the Civil War, a time of great social and political upheaval.

Exemplification of Perseverance: Lincoln faced numerous setbacks during his political career, including losing several elections. However, he never gave up on his vision of preserving the Union and abolishing slavery. Despite the personal, military, and political pressures, his perseverance through the Civil War was critical in maintaining the United States as one nation.

Impact on Others: Lincoln's determination and steadfast leadership inspired his contemporaries and future generations to commit to freedom, equality, and democracy. His speeches, such as the Gettysburg Address, motivate and move people globally.

These historical figures demonstrate that perseverance is not merely about persisting in the face of adversity; it's about transforming challenges into opportunities that lead to personal achievements and inspire and uplift others. Their legacies teach us the value of determination, courage, and the unrelenting pursuit of one's goals, no matter the odds.

"Block out the Noise"

Along the journey, there will be many who cast doubt on your success – you must ignore, block out and use this as motivation!

These people will try to derail you because:

1. Their jealousy
2. Their lack of achievements
3. Their lack of discipline

These are the people you never want to surround yourself with.

Why Perseverance Matters

1. Achieving Complex Goals

Most worthwhile goals require time, planning, and prolonged effort. Perseverance ensures that individuals continue to strive towards these goals, navigating through complexities and challenges that might otherwise derail their efforts.

2. Facing Failure with Strength

Failure is a natural part of the growth process. Perseverance enables individuals to learn from failures rather than be discouraged by them. This resilience is crucial for anyone navigating the unpredictable waters of innovation and competition.

3. Inspiring Others

Persevering can serve as a powerful example to others. Seeing one person persist in adversity in families, workplaces, and communities can encourage others to remain committed to their own goals, thereby creating a ripple effect of determination and resilience.

4. Building Character and Self-Respect

Consistently working towards a goal builds character, shaping a person into someone who can withstand difficulties. It also boosts self-respect, as individuals recognize their capacity to commit and endure.

Elements of Perseverance

- **Vision:** Strong, clear visions of achievements is essential. Vision guides the direction and fuels the motivation to persevere.

- **Motivation:** Internal motivation is a crucial driver of perseverance. It can stem from personal values, a desire to achieve, or pursuing a purpose.

- **Adaptability:** The ability to adapt strategies when faced with obstacles is crucial. Perseverance is not about stubbornly sticking to a failing plan but about persisting towards a goal, even if the path to get there needs to change.

- **Support Systems:** While perseverance is an individual effort, having a support system of friends, family, or colleagues can provide the external encouragement needed to continue.

Achieving Peace of Mind Through Perseverance in Life, Business, and Sports

Perseverance is a vital attribute that contributes significantly to achieving peace of mind across various facets of life, including personal endeavors, professional pursuits, and athletic achievements. Persevering embodies the determination to push through challenges and setbacks, transforming obstacles into opportunities for growth.

In life, individuals who persevere develop resilience, which fosters a sense of accomplishment and confidence, leading to overall contentment. In business, the ability to persist in the face of adversity often distinguishes successful leaders from those who falter, as it demonstrates commitment to goals and the capacity to adapt.

Similarly, athletes who embody perseverance cultivate mental fortitude, enabling them to overcome defeat and continuously strive for improvement. Ultimately, embracing perseverance propels individuals toward their objectives and instills a profound sense of tranquility and fulfillment, allowing them to embrace the journey rather than solely focusing on the destination.

Chapter 13

The Essence of Family

"Family is not an important thing. It's everything." — Michael J. Fox

The essence of family in contributing to one's success cannot be overstated. Famous individuals often emphasize the pivotal role that family plays as a foundation of support, inspiration, and strength.

Michael J. Fox's quote encapsulates this sentiment by highlighting how family serves as an integral pillar in navigating life's journey. With a nurturing family environment, individuals may feel empowered to pursue their dreams, take risks, and persevere through challenges. The bonds shared within a family instill confidence and resilience, offering emotional sustenance in both triumphant moments and times of adversity. In essence, family is often the unseen force propelling us towards realizing our potential and achieving success.

Family transcends the boundaries of mere biological or legal connections; it embodies the spirit of **unconditional** love, support, and belonging. Whether formed by blood, marriage, or choice, family means commitment and **nurtured** through love and respect.

Here are some key points highlighting its importance:

1. Support System

- **Emotional Support**: Family provides encouragement during tough times, boosting morale and resilience.
- **Safety Net**: A strong family serves as a safety net, allowing individuals to take risks in their careers or pursuits.

2. **Values and Ethics**

    - **Foundation of Values**: Family instills core values such as honesty, hard work, and integrity, which are essential in all aspects of life.

    - **Role Models**: Family members often serve as role models, demonstrating behaviors that lead to success.

3. **Collaboration and Teamwork**

    - **Shared Goals**: In business and sports, collaboration is key. Families often work together towards common goals, teaching teamwork.

    - **Conflict Resolution**: Navigating disagreements within a family can enhance conflict resolution skills, beneficial in professional and athletic settings.

4. **Networking and Opportunities**

    - **Connections**: Family can provide valuable connections and networking opportunities in business and sports.

    - **Resource Sharing**: Access to resources and knowledge from family members may open doors to new opportunities.

5. **Work-Life Balance**

    - **Prioritizing Relationships**: A strong family encourages individuals to maintain a healthy work-life balance, which is crucial for long-term success.

    - **Mental Well-Being**: Family relationships contribute to overall happiness, which can enhance performance in business and sports.

6. **Motivation and Accountability**

   - **Inspiration**: Family members often motivate each other to strive for excellence and achieve personal goals.

   - **Accountability**: A supportive family can hold individuals accountable, helping them stay focused on their objectives.

The Roles and Functions of Family

1. **Emotional Support:** Families provide a safety net of emotional support. Family members offer each other an irreplaceable source of comfort and encouragement, from the joyous celebrations of life's milestones to the comforting embrace in times of despair.

2. **Social Development:** The family is the first social structure that individuals encounter. It is where children learn the values of trust, empathy, cooperation, and respect. These early lessons profoundly influence their future interactions and the formation of their moral compass.

3. **Economic Support:** Families often function as economic units that support each member. From pooling resources to help one another's education to aid in financial distress, the economic interdependence within families fosters survival and prosperity.

4. **Cultural Transmission:** Families are also the primary conduit for passing down cultural traditions and values. Through stories, rituals, and daily habits, children absorb the heritage of their predecessors, creating a sense of identity and continuity.

Challenges Facing Modern Families

In today's rapidly changing world, families face numerous challenges that test their strength and unity. However, it's important to remember that families are remarkably resilient, and with the right strategies, they can overcome these challenges.

- **Time Constraints:** With the demands of modern careers and the fast pace of life, finding quality time for family can be challenging. This can strain the relationship and weaken the bond.

- **Geographical Separation:** Globalization and pursuing career opportunities can lead to geographical spread, making it hard to maintain close family ties.

- **Economic Pressures:** Financial instability can create significant stress within families, sometimes leading to conflict and alienation.

- **Cultural Shifts:** As societies evolve, traditional family structures and roles within them challenge previously accepted norms and expectations.

Strengthening Family Bonds

Despite these challenges, the fundamental value of family remains unchanged. Strengthening family bonds requires intentional efforts:

- **Quality Time:** Prioritizing regular family gatherings, such as meals or outings, can help reinforce bonds. These moments are not just opportunities for members to connect, but they also inspire and motivate each other, fostering a stronger family unit.

- **Communication:** Encouraging honest and open communication is a powerful tool in addressing misunderstandings and conflicts before they escalate, empowering each family member to take control of their relationships and fostering a healthier family dynamic.

- **Support and Respect:** Recognizing and supporting each other's ambitions and challenges reinforces mutual respect and love, which are vital for a robust family unit.

- **Adaptation and Flexibility:** Embracing changes and adapting to new family dynamics (such as marriages, births, or elderly care) is crucial for maintaining harmony and unity.

Challenges of Maintaining Family Unity in Modern Society

In a world where both the pace and landscape of life are changing rapidly, maintaining family unity presents a complex set of challenges. However, the family unit, with its resilience and adaptability, remains a crucial anchor in the face of these changes. Technological advancements, cultural shifts, and evolving societal norms have significantly reshaped the dynamics of family life. This exploration will delve into the key challenges that modern families face in preserving their unity and cohesion amidst these changes.

1. Blurring of Traditional Roles

Overview:
Traditional family roles have been clearly defined for generations. Still, modern society has shifted towards more fluid and less prescriptive roles within the family. While this has many positive aspects, including promoting gender equality and personal fulfillment, it can lead to confusion and conflict as family members navigate new expectations and responsibilities.

Impact:
- **Role Confusion:** As traditional roles become less defined, family members may need help with who is responsible for specific tasks or decision-making, potentially leading to conflicts.

- **Resentment:** Adjusting to new roles may create tension, especially if the change is not universally accepted within the family.

2. Digital Distraction and Communication Barriers

Overview:
Social Media has transformed how we communicate, offering new ways to connect and creating barriers to face-to-face interaction. The prevalence of smartphones, tablets, and computers can significantly detract from quality family time.

Impact:
- **Reduced Face-to-Face Interaction:** Excessive screen time can reduce opportunities for meaningful personal interactions, which are crucial for maintaining emotional bonds.

- **Miscommunications:** Digital communication lacks the nuances of face-to-face conversation, such as body language and tone, which can lead to misunderstandings.

3. Economic Pressures

Overview:
Modern families often face significant economic pressures, including the high cost of living, job insecurity, and the need for dual incomes to sustain a household. These pressures can strain family relationships, especially when coupled with limited time for family interaction.

Impact:
- **Stress and Conflict:** Financial stress can lead to discord and strain in relationships, as family members may be less emotionally available and more prone to conflict.

- **Limited Quality Time:** Work demands can encroach on family time, making it challenging to nurture relationships and maintain a sense of unity.

4. Geographical Separation

Overview:
Globalization and job opportunities can lead families to live apart and spread across cities or continents. This geographical separation poses significant challenges to maintaining family unity.

Impact:
- **Weakening of Bonds:** Physical distance can weaken familial bonds, as members miss out on daily interactions and shared experiences.

- **Dependency on Technology for Communication:** While technology can help bridge the gap, physical presence is often a substitute for physical presence, especially during significant life events or crises.

Strategies for Overcoming Challenges

Maintaining family unity in the face of these challenges requires intentional strategies. Among these, open and frequent communication stands out as a key tool. Encouraging regular family meetings to discuss roles, expectations, and issues can foster understanding and unity within the family.

- **Open and Frequent Communication:** Encourage regular family meetings to discuss roles, expectations, and issues.

- **Another Crucial Strategy** for maintaining family unity is to prioritize quality time together without digital distractions. Regular family meals or outings, where the focus is on personal interaction rather than screen time, can significantly contribute to fostering emotional bonds and unity within the family.

- **Flexibility and Adaptation:** Be open to evolving family roles and responsibilities, adapting as needed to accommodate changes in the family structure or individual needs.

- **Financial Planning:** Work together on financial planning and budgeting to reduce economic stress and ensure all family members are on the same page.

- **Cultural Sensitivity and Education:** Embrace and celebrate cultural diversity within the family and educate each member about different cultural backgrounds to foster understanding and respect.

Achieving Peace of Mind as a Family in Life, Business, and Sports

In summary, the essence of family is pivotal for success across various domains. The support, values, collaboration, opportunities, balance, and motivation that family provides create a solid foundation for individuals to thrive in life, business, and sports.

Family shapes our identities, supports our endeavors, and provides a framework for understanding the world. In recognizing and nurturing the value of family, we enhance our personal lives and contribute to a stronger, more compassionate society. Let us cherish and uphold the sanctity of family, for in its strength lies the health and happiness of our communities and future generations.

Chapter 14

Embracing Failure as a Stepping Stone to Success

"I can accept failure. Everyone fails at something. But I can't accept not trying. Obstacles don't have to stop you. If you run into a wall, don't turn around and give up. Figure out how to climb it, go through it, or work around it." - Michael Jordan

Failure, though often feared and misunderstood, is an inevitable part of life's journey. Whether in personal growth, business ventures, or competitive sports, failure is not the end; rather, it is the beginning of learning, growth, and eventual triumph. This chapter explores how failure serves as a vital stepping stone to success across various domains of life.

Failure in Life: A Catalyst for Growth

In life, failure is a teacher, not a tormentor. Each failed attempt at something offers valuable lessons that shape our character, fortify our resilience, and refine our strategies.

- **Learning from Mistakes**: When we fail, we gain a clearer understanding of what doesn't work. For instance, a student failing an exam may realize they need to alter their study techniques or manage their time better. This newfound awareness becomes the foundation for future success.

- **Building Resilience**: Failure teaches us how to adapt to challenges. Life is unpredictable, and the ability to bounce back from setbacks is essential for long-term happiness. Resilience, cultivated through failure, enables us to face adversity with confidence.

- **Discovering New Paths**: Sometimes, failure redirects us toward better opportunities. For example, someone failing at one career might discover untapped talents in another field, leading to success they never thought possible.

Failure, then, is not an obstacle but an opportunity—a chance to evolve into a stronger, wiser version of ourselves.

Failure in Business: The Road to Innovation

In the world of business, failure is often seen as a prerequisite for success. Many of the most successful entrepreneurs and companies owe their achievements to lessons learned from failed ventures.

- **Innovation Through Experimentation**: Thomas Edison, one of history's greatest inventors, famously said, "I have not failed. I've just found 10,000 ways that won't work." His relentless experimentation eventually led to the invention of the light bulb. In business, failure during experimentation often paves the way for breakthroughs.

- **Case Studies of Success After Failure**: Steve Jobs is a prime example. After being ousted from Apple, the company he co-founded, he used the "failure" as fuel to innovate further, eventually returning to Apple and transforming it into one of the most valuable companies in the world.

- **Risk and Reward**: Every business venture involves risk, and not all risks will pay off. However, each failure provides critical insights into market demands, customer preferences, and operational inefficiencies. Entrepreneurs who embrace failure as feedback are better equipped to succeed in the long run.

Failure in business is not a sign of defeat; it is a stepping stone that entrepreneurs and organizations use to climb higher.

Failure in Sports: The Path to Greatness

Sports, perhaps more than any other domain, vividly illustrate the transformative power of failure. Athletes experience constant setbacks, yet their perseverance and determination often lead them to greatness.

- **Training Through Trial and Error**: Athletes frequently fail in practice before they succeed in competition. A basketball player may miss countless free throws in training, but through persistence and adjustment, they perfect their technique. Every missed shot is a step closer to mastery.

- **Iconic Comebacks**: Michael Jordan, widely regarded as one of the greatest basketball players of all time, has said, "I've missed more than 9,000 shots in my career. I've lost almost 300 games. I've failed over and over and over again in my life. And that is why I succeed." His failures on the court fueled his work ethic and hunger for success.

- **Mental Toughness**: Failure in sports teaches athletes to overcome disappointment and keep pushing forward. It builds the mental toughness necessary to perform under pressure, a quality that sets champions apart.

In sports, failure is not the end of the game; it is the beginning of the journey toward excellence.

Why Failure is Essential for Success

Across life, business, and sports, failure shares a common thread: it forces us to confront our weaknesses and grow stronger. Without failure, there would be no learning, no innovation, and no triumph.

- **Failure Builds Character**: The humility and perseverance developed through failure shape our character. It teaches us to stay grounded in victory and optimistic in defeat.

- **Failure Fuels Motivation**: The sting of failure can ignite a burning desire to improve. It pushes us to work harder, think smarter, and strive for greatness.

- **Failure Redefines Success**: Success achieved without failure often feels hollow. The struggles and setbacks along the way make success more meaningful and rewarding.

Embracing Failure

To harness the power of failure, we must change our perspective. Instead of fearing failure, we should welcome it as a necessary step in the journey to success. Here are some strategies to embrace failure:

1. **View Failure as Feedback**: Each failure provides valuable information about what works and what doesn't.

2. **Celebrate Effort**: Acknowledge the courage it takes to try, even if the outcome isn't as expected.

3. **Stay Persistent**: Remember that success often requires multiple attempts. Keep going, even when the road is difficult.

Achieving Peace of Mind Through Embracing Failure as a Stepping Stone to Success

Failure is not the opposite of success; it is an integral part of it. In life, business, and sports, failure challenges us, teaches us, and prepares us for the victories to come. By embracing failure as a stepping stone, we unlock our full potential and achieve greatness. So, the next time you stumble, remember failure is not the end—it is the beginning of success.

Chapter 15

Accountability

The concept of accountability also plays a significant role in success, as it involves taking ownership of one's actions and outcomes. Many successful individuals have stressed the importance of personal accountability, such as **Oprah Winfrey** who said, *"I don't think you ever stop giving. I really don't. I think it's an ongoing process. And it's not just about being able to write a check. It's being able to touch somebody's life."* This quote exemplifies how taking responsibility for one's actions can lead to positive impact on others.

I always interview parents before I decide to work with their children. If the parents are complaining about the coaches, teachers and administrators, I will not work with the student athlete unfortunately. Parents must teach their children to be accountable and not blame others.

Accountability is the personal commitment to owning one's actions and outcomes, as well as the responsibilities assigned to oneself. It is about being reliable and transparent, facing the consequences of one's actions without resorting to excuses or shifting blame onto others. When individuals embrace accountability, they enhance their credibility and trustworthiness in personal and professional settings. This commitment involves a straightforward acceptance of success and failures, using each as a stepping-stone for personal growth and improvement. By fostering an environment where accountability is valued, organizations and relationships can thrive, obstacles can be navigated more effectively, and a culture of mutual respect and continuous learning can be cultivated. This enlightenment about the power of accountability can empower individuals to take control of their actions and decisions, leading to personal and professional growth.

Hypothetical Scenario: Business Project Management

Situation:

John, a project manager in a software development company, was leading a team on a critical project with a tight deadline. Despite careful planning, the project encountered significant delays due to unforeseen technical challenges and some initial underestimation of the task's complexity.

Accountability Demonstration:

Realizing the project needed to catch up, John convened a meeting with his team and stakeholders. In this meeting, he openly acknowledged his oversight in the initial project scope and underestimated timelines. He clearly assessed the current situation without blaming his team or external factors for the setbacks.

Action Taken:

John proposed a revised plan to expedite the project's completion. The new plan involved reallocating resources, introducing additional shifts, and requesting temporary external expertise to address specific technical challenges. He communicated these changes transparently with his team. He involved them in decision-making to ensure everyone was on board and understood their roles.

Positive Impact:

John's accountability not only salvaged the project but also fostered a supportive team environment. His transparency and willingness to own up to mistakes increased his team's trust and respect towards him. It encouraged similar honesty among team members, who began to communicate more openly about potential issues or delays. This shift facilitated faster problem-solving and boosted team morale, as members felt more involved and valued. Ultimately, John completed the project close to the new timeline, and the client appreciated the clear communication and quality of work, leading to more business opportunities. This success story serves as an inspiration for all of us, showing the transformative power of accountability in leadership.

Conclusion:

In this scenario, John's demonstration of accountability helped to turn a potentially harmful situation into a successful outcome by fostering a culture of trust, open communication, and collaborative problem-solving. His approach salvaged the project and strengthened his team's cohesion and resilience, proving that accountability is crucial in leadership for immediate and long-term success.

Fostering a culture of accountability within a team is crucial for achieving high performance and maintaining a harmonious and productive work environment. Here are several best practices that can help establish and nurture this culture:

Hypothetical Scenario: Accountability in Sports

Situation:

Athletes with accountability do their jobs – they work hard, go to class, perform well in the classroom, complete their offseason training, act responsibly in their social lives – all without someone begging them to do it or needing to watch over them 24/7.

Accountability Demonstration: Six examples

- Recognize and own the power of their choices, decisions and actions.

- Consciously and consistently make helpful choices and minimize hurtful choices

- Discipline themselves daily so others don't have to
- Control the controllable
- Own and learn from your mistakes
- Follow through and finish the job

Action Taken:

Cassidy's outstanding work ethic with our team has made a significant difference in our program

Positive Impact:

Cassidy's accountability not only salvaged the season but also fostered a supportive team environment. Her transparency and willingness to own up to mistakes increased her team's trust and respect towards her. This success story serves as an inspiration for all of us, showing the transformative power of accountability in leadership.

Conclusion:

In this scenario, Cassidy's demonstration of accountability helped to turn a potentially losing season into a championship team.

Accountability Guidelines in Life

Set Clear Expectations

Define Roles and Responsibilities

- Ensure every team member clearly understands their roles and the expectations associated with their tasks. Detailed job descriptions and regular discussions can clarify any ambiguities.

Establish Goals

- Set specific, measurable, achievable, relevant, and time-bound (SMART) goals that align with the team's and organization's objectives.

Provide the Necessary Resources

- Ensure team members have the tools, training, and support to meet their responsibilities. This includes access to technology, educational opportunities, and managerial support.

Create an Open Communication Environment

Encourage Transparency

- Promote an open-door policy where team members feel comfortable discussing successes, setbacks, and concerns without fear of negative repercussions.

Regular Feedback

- Implement a system of regular, constructive feedback, which should not only come from the top down but also encourage peer-to-peer feedback.

Lead by Example

- Leaders should model the accountability they expect in their team members, including admitting mistakes, celebrating successes, and following through on commitments. When leaders act with integrity and responsibility, it sets a powerful example for the entire team.

Implement Accountability Structures

Use Accountability Frameworks

- Tools like RACI charts (Responsible, Accountable, Consulted, and Informed) can help clarify who is accountable for different tasks and outcomes.

Regular Check-Ins

- Hold meetings to review progress on goals and address any issues to keep everyone informed and responsible.

Recognize and Reward Accountability

- Publicly acknowledge and reward behaviors demonstrating accountability through formal recognition programs, bonuses, or simple public acknowledgment in meetings. Positive reinforcement can motivate others to act similarly.

Deal with Accountability Issues Promptly

- Address failures to meet commitments or poor performance promptly and constructively. Ignoring such issues can undermine a culture of accountability. Ensure that the focus is on finding solutions and learning from mistakes rather than punishing individuals.

Foster a Learning Environment

- Promote a mindset that views setbacks as learning opportunities. Encourage team members to analyze what went wrong and how similar mistakes can be avoided in the future rather than focusing solely on the failure.

Encourage Ownership and Autonomy

- Empower team members by giving them ownership of their tasks and the authority to make decisions relevant to their roles. Autonomy can enhance a sense of responsibility and accountability.

Build Mutual Trust

- Trust is fundamental to accountability. Build trust through consistent actions, reliability, and fairness in handling all team interactions.

Peace of Mind Through Accountability in Life, Business, and Sports

Accountability plays a crucial role in achieving peace of mind across various aspects of life, including personal relationships, professional environments, and athletic pursuits. When individuals take responsibility for their actions and decisions, they foster a sense of ownership, leading to greater clarity and control over their circumstances. Accountability enhances communication and trust in personal relationships, allowing for deeper connections and understanding. In business, accountability encourages transparency and team cohesion, ultimately driving performance and innovation. For athletes, taking responsibility for their training and competition outcomes helps cultivate a disciplined mindset, allowing them to focus on continuous improvement. This reassurance that accountability brings can instill a sense of confidence in individuals, knowing that they have the power to shape their own outcomes.

Chapter 16

Don't Waste Energy

"Waste no more time arguing what a good man should be. Be One."
- Marcus Aurelius

This philosophical perspective encourages immediate action and energy conservation, urging us to focus on being our best selves rather than wasting energy on endless debates.

Focusing one's energy on aspects of life within one's control, rather than expending it on what cannot be influenced, is crucial for maintaining mental and emotional well-being. This approach leads to greater productivity and satisfaction, channeling efforts towards actionable and impactful activities.

Manage TIME not WORK

- The most valuable item to give your team is your time.

- There are only 24 hours in a day, therefore, you must learn to prioritize your tasks-determine which are most important and critical to the company.

- As the leader, you must spend most of the time focusing on the BIG picture and not the everyday operational details

- Every day operational details must be handled by your managers or assistants—these MUST not be allowed to bog you down

Stop Wasting Your Energy on Toxic People:

1. Identify the toxic people in your life.
2. Stop listening to their complaints.
3. Drown them with positivity.
4. Don't spend one-on-one time with them.
5. Don't take it personally.
6. Have some self-respect.
7. Surround yourself with positive people.
8. Stop spending time with them.

Business

Consider the example of Maria, a project manager in a bustling technology firm. Maria often found herself stressed and overwhelmed by deadlines and the unpredictable dynamics of her team members' performance, which she felt were beyond her control. Realizing the toll this stress took on her health and job satisfaction, Maria shifted her focus to factors within her control.

Firstly, Maria began by enhancing her own time management and organizational skills. She adopted new productivity tools and techniques, such as the Eisenhower Box, to prioritize tasks and block specific times for deep work, allowing her to manage her workload more effectively and reduce procrastination.

Secondly, Maria focused on improving her communication and leadership skills. She started regular one-on-one meetings with her team members to understand their challenges and motivations better, thus enabling her to provide more tailored support and guidance, fostering a more productive and cohesive team environment.

Lastly, Maria implemented stress-reduction techniques into her daily routine. She started practicing mindfulness meditation during breaks and encouraged a team culture where taking short; regular breaks were normalized to maintain mental clarity and reduce burnout.

By concentrating her efforts on these controllable aspects of her work life, Maria experienced significant improvements. Her project completion rates improved, team morale boosted, and she reported higher job satisfaction and lower stress levels. This shift made her a more effective leader. It enhanced her well-being, demonstrating the profound impact of focusing on controllable factors. The sense of achievement and satisfaction that Maria felt from these improvements is a testament to the power of this approach.

Life

Applying the principles of focusing on controllable factors can significantly enhance personal relationships. Here's how one might do it:

1. Improve Communication Skills

- **Control:** You can control how openly and effectively you communicate with others. Work on being a better listener, expressing your feelings clearly, and addressing conflicts constructively.

- **Impact:** Improved communication reduces misunderstandings and builds trust, making relationships more robust and resilient.

2. Manage Reactions and Emotions

- **Control:** While you can't control others' actions or feelings, you can control your reactions. Learn to manage your emotional responses through deep breathing, mindfulness, or pausing before responding in heated situations.

- **Impact:** This helps maintain harmony and prevents escalation of conflicts, promoting a peaceful and supportive relationship environment.

3. Set and Respect Boundaries

- **Control:** You have the power to set personal boundaries about what is acceptable behavior and what isn't. Equally, you can respect others' boundaries, acknowledging their right to personal space and privacy.

- **Impact:** Boundaries help define the health and sustainability of relationships, ensuring mutual respect and understanding.

4. Increase Reliability

- **Control:** Being reliable—showing up on time, keeping promises, and being consistent—is within your control.

- **Impact:** Reliability builds trust and shows commitment, which is foundational to any strong relationship.

5. Focus on Positive Actions

- **Control:** You can focus on positive actions, such as showing appreciation, supporting during tough times, and celebrating successes together.

- **Impact:** Positive reinforcement strengthens bonds and enhances mutual joy and satisfaction in relationships.

6. Personal Development

- Invest in personal growth—learning new things, improving your health, or cultivating new hobbies.

<u>Sports</u>

Athletes are able to perform at high levels for extended periods without getting as tired as the average person does due to several physiological adaptations and training techniques:

1. Cardiovascular Fitness: Regular training increases the efficiency of the heart and lungs, allowing for better oxygen delivery to working muscles. This enhanced cardiovascular fitness delays the onset of fatigue.

2. Muscle Adaptations: Intense training leads to increases in muscle size, strength, and endurance. Muscles become better able to use oxygen and clear lactic acid, reducing the buildup of fatigue-inducing metabolites.

3. Fuel Storage and Utilization: Training causes the body to store more glycogen (the body's preferred fuel) in muscle and liver, as well as improving the body's ability to access and use fat as fuel. This allows players to maintain energy levels for longer.

4. Cooling Mechanisms: Athletes' bodies become better at regulating temperature through sweating and other heat dissipation processes, preventing overheating which can lead to fatigue.

5. Psychological Factors: Elite athletes develop mental toughness and strategies to push through discomfort and perceived fatigue. Motivation, focus, and pain tolerance all play a role.

6. Recovery and Adaptation: Proper nutrition, hydration, and rest between training and competition allows the body to recover and adapt, minimizing the cumulative effects of fatigue.

The combination of these physiological and psychological adaptations is what enables top athletes to sustain high-intensity physical activity for extended durations without succumbing to debilitating levels of fatigue.

Not Wasting Valuable Energy Achieves Peace of Mind in Life, Business, and Sports

Absolutely! Not wasting valuable energy can significantly contribute to achieving peace of mind.

Life

- **Mental Clarity**: By focusing only on what truly matters, you reduce stress and anxiety.
- **Balanced Living**: Prioritizing energy-efficient practices allows for a more balanced approach to work and personal life.

Business

- **Efficiency**: Streamlining processes and eliminating waste leads to better productivity and profitability.
- **Sustainable Practices**: Companies that prioritize energy conservation often enjoy a positive reputation and customer loyalty.

Sports

- **Optimal Performance**: Athletes who conserve energy through smart training and technique can enhance their performance.

- **Mental Focus**: Reducing distractions helps athletes maintain concentration and achieve their goals.

In all these areas, being mindful of energy usage fosters a sense of control and tranquility, leading to improved outcomes and well-being.

Chapter 17

The Benefits of a Great Partner

A great relationship is about two things: first, appreciating the similarities and second, respecting the differences." — **Michelle Obama**

A great partner has the power to profoundly transform your life, serving as a pillar of support, a confidant, and a source of inspiration. They provide emotional stability, making you feel valued and understood which boosts your self-esteem and overall happiness. A great partner will present you with a different perspective on life then what you grew up with—not necessarily better – but different. These perspectives more than likely are not what you may have thought of in life, business and sports.

In **life**, a supportive spouse is an invaluable asset in various facets of life, including personal relationships, business, and sports. They provide emotional strength and stability, allowing individuals to confidently navigate life's challenges. This partnership cultivates a home environment rich in encouragement, where both parties feel empowered to pursue their goals.

In **business**, a spouse can offer unique insights and perspectives, drawing from their experiences to enhance decision-making and strategic planning. They can serve as a sounding board for ideas and provide constructive feedback, facilitating personal and professional growth. Their network may also open doors to opportunities that would otherwise remain inaccessible. This role of a supportive spouse in personal growth can empower and motivate you in your own relationship.

Regarding **sports**, having the right spouse can ignite passion and commitment to fitness and well-being. They can participate in physical activities together, fostering motivation and accountability. Whether cheering from the sidelines or training together, their support can significantly affect performance and overall enjoyment. This multifaceted support reinforces the idea that a solid marital partnership is about love and collaboration in all areas of life.

Personal Experiences Highlight the Benefits of Partnership for Life

My marriage is a prime example when reflecting on the importance of partnership. Having my spouse by my side has made an extraordinary difference throughout various challenges, whether personal struggles or family decisions. We approach each hurdle as a united front, celebrating our victories, no matter how small, and comforting each other during tough times. This mutual support fosters a deep emotional bond that strengthens our relationship.

Moreover, the ability to share dreams and aspirations is a unique aspect of our partnership. We encourage each other to pursue our passions, whether embarking on a new venture or nurturing a hobby. This unwavering support builds individual confidence and enhances our connection, making our marriage a shared journey filled with growth and joy. Our marital partnership blossoms through laughter, teamwork, and resilience, proving that true companionship enriches life in immeasurable ways.

For men, a robust theory exists that a married man will live much longer.

Embracing vulnerability is also crucial; sharing fears, insecurities, and ambitions can deepen the emotional connection and promote a sense of solidarity. By acknowledging each other's contributions and celebrating achievements, practicing gratitude further cultivates a positive environment. Ultimately, achieving peace of mind in a marriage is about creating a nurturing atmosphere where both partners feel valued, supported, and loved, paving the way for lasting harmony and fulfillment.

Here are a few real-life examples that illustrate how shared values and goals can strengthen relationships:

Example 1: Commitment to Family

John and Sarah grew up in close-knit families and shared a substantial value for family connections. When they married, they prioritized creating a nurturing environment for their children and ensuring strong bonds with extended family members. Their shared commitment to family meant they supported each other in making career decisions that allowed for family time and involved their children in regular gatherings with relatives. This shared value deepened their bond and provided a stable and loving environment for their children.

Example 2: Passion for Philanthropy

Mike and Linda met during a volunteer event and discovered a mutual passion for philanthropy and community service. They engaged in various charitable activities as a couple, eventually starting a non-profit organization together. Their shared goal of helping others not only brought them closer but also gave them a fulfilling and meaningful shared purpose, strengthening their relationship as they worked together towards a common cause.

Example 3: Love for Adventure

When they met, **Alex and Jamie** both had a thirst for adventure and a love for travel. They made it their mutual goal to visit every country in the world. Each trip they planned and executed together reinforced their bond, taught them new ways to rely on each other, and enriched their experiences and understanding of the world. Their shared value of adventure kept their relationship dynamic and exciting.

Example 4: Environmental Advocacy

Emma and Raj shared a solid commitment to environmental sustainability, which influenced their lifestyle choices—from the products they bought and the food they ate to how they managed their homes. They worked together on various environmental projects, including building a sustainable home and advocating for local green initiatives. This shared value aligned them on daily living practices and made them partners in a cause they were both passionate about.

Example 5: Lifelong Learning

Chloe and Ethan both valued education and lifelong learning. They supported each other's educational pursuits and career advancements, regularly attended workshops and lectures together, and set aside time each week to teach each other something new. This commitment to growth and learning kept their relationship intellectually stimulating and emotionally supportive.

In each case, the couples had significant shared values or goals that acted as glue, keeping them aligned and focused on common objectives. These shared aspects provided a foundation of understanding and mutual respect, essential for a robust and lasting relationship. This emphasis on the importance of shared values and goals can inspire and encourage you in your own relationship.

If You're Not Receiving the Support You Need from Your Spouse, Consider the Following Enlightening Solutions:

Read the book *The 5 Love Languages* by Gary Chapman - fun and insightful:

Falling in love is easy. Staying in love—that's the challenge. How can you keep your relationship fresh and growing amid everyday life's demands, conflicts, and just plain boredom?

This test can be fun and enlightening. You may have thought your wife's love language was "acts of service" by performing chores around the house for years. After taking this test, you realize your wife's love language is "quality time," she wants to spend time with you on dates, teatime, and romantic dinners.

Take the Color Test to Determine Your and Your Partner's Personality.

This test relies on preference to assess various aspects of your unique personality, including your goals, anxieties, needs, and motivation. It is important to remember that this test is not meant to be taken as a definitive assessment of who you are, but it is another way to learn about yourself and your partner.

Key Points to Never Stop Working On with Your Partner:

1. **Open Communication**: Share your feelings with your partner honestly and calmly. Let them know what support you need.

2. **Set Clear Expectations**: Discuss what emotional support means to you. This will clarify needs and avoid misunderstandings.

3. **Seek Professional Help**: Consider entering into couples therapy or counseling to facilitate better communication skills and understanding between you.

4. **Practice Self-Care**: Focus on your emotional well-being. Engage in activities that bring you joy and fulfillment outside the marriage.

5. **Build a Support Network**: Try to cultivate friendships and relationships outside your marriage for emotional support. This can help alleviate some pressure on your partner.

6. **Encourage Vulnerability**: Foster an environment where both partners feel safe to express their vulnerabilities, fears, and desires.

7. **Be Patient**: Understand that change takes time. Be patient with your partner as they adjust to your needs.

8. **Prioritize Quality Time**: Spend dedicated time together to strengthen your emotional connection and rekindle intimacy.

9. **Express Appreciation**: Acknowledge and celebrate your spouse's efforts towards supporting you, no matter how small.

10. **Reassess the Relationship**: If emotional support continues to be a significant issue, it may be necessary to evaluate the relationship's overall health and consider what changes are needed, possibly break up, and find a better partner.

11. **Respect and Love**: Typically, in a relationship, a man seeks his wife to respect his efforts and skillset. At the same time, a woman yearns for his love. Knowing this fact, both partners must create a mindset for this culture to exist, grow and prosper.

Achieving Peace of Mind with Your Partner in Life, Business, and Sports

Achieving peace of mind with your partner requires intentional effort and open communication. Establishing a safe space where both partners can express their thoughts and feelings without judgment fosters trust and understanding. Regularly checking in with each other about emotional well-being, concerns, and expectations can help prevent misunderstandings and build a solid foundation of support. Additionally, practices such as setting aside dedicated time for each other, tea time, date nights or quiet evenings at home, can serve as a reminder of the partnership's significance, allowing both partners to reconnect and recharge.

Chapter 18

Living a Healthy Life

"Investing in yourself is the best investment you will ever make. It will not only improve your life, but it will also improve the lives of all those around you." - Robin Sharma

Self-care is not selfish. Taking care of ourselves allows us to show up as our best selves in all areas of our lives, including relationships and work.

Living a healthy life usually requires a balanced lifestyle. When my children were little, I would put my weekly schedule together every Sunday. I would always insert my workouts first – maintaining my health was #1 to continue being a husband, father, entrepreneur and athlete. Next, I would schedule my weekly date with my wife and then fill in family activities. School functions were the next on the list, and after all those were in my schedule, I would begin my weekly work schedule with appointments. Amazingly, everything always worked out, and I was able to live a much more balanced and healthy life.

Living a healthy life involves a holistic approach that encompasses mental well-being and a nutritious diet.

Life

1. **Balanced Nutrition**: Eating a well-balanced diet rich in fruits, vegetables, whole grains, and lean proteins fuels the body and mind.

2. **Regular Exercise**: Engaging in physical activities, whether it's yoga, running, or team sports, enhances mood and energy levels.

3. **Mental Health**: Practices like mindfulness and meditation can reduce stress and improve focus, leading to better decision-making.

4. **Sleep Hygiene**: Prioritizing quality sleep helps in recovery and cognitive function, essential for daily tasks and responsibilities.

Business

1. **Work-Life Balance**: Maintaining boundaries between work and personal life is crucial for long-term productivity and creativity.

2. **Healthy Work Environment**: Fostering a culture of wellness in the workplace can enhance teamwork and morale.

3. **Stress Management**: Implementing various stress-reduction techniques, such as regular breaks and wellness programs, can lead to higher performance.

4. **Continuous Learning**: Staying curious and open to new ideas contributes to personal and professional growth.

Sports

1. **Physical Conditioning**: Athletes need to focus on strength, endurance, and flexibility to perform at their best.

2. **Nutrition for Performance**: Tailoring diets to meet the demands of training and competition is vital for optimal performance.

3. **Mental Toughness**: Developing mental resilience through visualization and goal-setting helps athletes overcome challenges.

4. **Team Dynamics**: Building strong relationships with teammates fosters collaboration and enhances overall performance.

Healthy Eating

Making healthy eating enjoyable and sustainable involves integrating it seamlessly into your lifestyle while ensuring it remains exciting and satisfying. Here are several strategies to help you achieve this:

1. **Explore New Recipes**

   One of the most exciting aspects of healthy eating is the opportunity to discover new recipes. Regularly exploring cuisines from different cultures, each with their unique blend of spices and ingredients can be a delightful journey. Websites, apps, and cookbooks are treasure troves of healthy recipes waiting to be unearthed.

2. **Cook with Others**

   One of the best ways to make cooking a more enjoyable experience is by sharing it with friends or family members. This not only makes the process more fun but also provides a platform to learn new techniques and ideas from each other. It's a social event that can bring everyone closer together, enhancing the enjoyment of the meal.

3. **Focus on Flavor**

   Use herbs, spices, and seasonings to enhance the flavor of your meals without adding extra calories. Experimenting with flavor combinations can transform your dishes and make healthy ingredients more palatable and exciting.

4. **Plan Your Meals**

   Meal planning can reduce the stress of deciding what to eat daily and help you maintain a balanced diet. Plan your weekly meals, including snacks, and grocery shop accordingly. This helps minimize the temptation to opt for less healthy, more convenient options.

5. **Grow Your Ingredients**

   Start a small garden to grow your herbs, vegetables, or fruits. Gardening can be a relaxing and rewarding hobby, and using your home-grown produce in your cooking can make meals more memorable and enjoyable.

6. **Make Healthy Swaps**

   Find healthier alternatives to your favorite dishes. For example, use whole-grain pasta instead of refined pasta or add grated vegetables to sauces and baked goods to enhance nutritional content without sacrificing taste.

7. **Eat Seasonally**

   Eating fruits and vegetables in season ensures better taste and freshness and can be more cost-effective. Seasonal eating also adds natural variety to your diet throughout the year.

8. **Involve All Senses**

   Make your meals visually appealing. The appearance of food can significantly influence your desire to eat it. Use colorful vegetables and thoughtful plating to make your dishes as beautiful as they are nutritious.

9. **Mindful Eating**

   Pay attention to what and how you eat. Eat slowly and savor each bite, which can increase your enjoyment of food and help you recognize when you are full, reducing the likelihood of overeating.

10. **Keep Snacks Interesting**

    Prepare a variety of healthy snacks that are ready to eat. Options like sliced fruits, nuts, yogurt, or homemade granola bars can be convenient and satisfying.

By incorporating these strategies, you can make healthy eating more enjoyable and integral to your daily routine, leading to a more sustainable and pleasurable approach to maintaining your health.

Healthy Mind

Establishing a sustainable routine to maintain both a healthy mind and body involves creating habits that are both effective and enjoyable, ensuring longevity and adherence over time. Here are some practical strategies to help you build a routine that lasts:

1. **Set Realistic Goals**

   Start with clear, achievable goals that motivate you. Small, incremental changes are more sustainable than drastic alterations. For instance, aim to add more vegetables to your meals gradually or introduce 10 minutes of meditation into your daily routine before scaling up.

2. **Incorporate Variety**

   Mix up your activities and diet to avoid monotony. Trying different physical activities (yoga, hiking, swimming, strength training) can keep you engaged and prevent burnout. Similarly, experimenting with diverse cuisines can make healthy eating enjoyable and less of a chore.

3. **Create a Schedule**

   Consistency is vital in forming lasting habits. Plan specific times for your activities, like setting aside time for exercise in the morning or meditation before bed. Treat these times as fixed appointments.

4. **Use Technology**
   Leverage apps and devices to track your progress, set reminders, or guide you through workouts and meditation sessions. These tools can provide structure and feedback, enhancing your motivation and adherence to your routine.

5. **Build a Support Network**

   Surround yourself with people who share your health goals. Join groups, classes, or online communities where members encourage and inspire each other. Having support can make the journey more enjoyable and less daunting.

6. **Listen to Your Body**

   Pay attention to how your body and mind respond to different activities and diets. Adjust your routine based on what makes you feel good and what doesn't. This personalization is crucial for long-term sustainability.

7. **Prioritize Sleep**

   Ensure you get enough restful sleep, as it affects both mental and physical health. Establish a calming bedtime routine and a sleep-friendly environment to improve sleep quality.

8. **Practice Mindfulness**

   Incorporate mindfulness into your daily life as a separate activity and a way of being. This could mean mindful eating, mindful walking, or simply being present at the moment during various activities.

9. **Reward Progress**

   Acknowledge and celebrate your achievements, no matter how small. For example, you could treat yourself to a massage after completing a week of workouts or a small social outing after maintaining your diet. Rewards can reinforce positive behavior.

10. **Be Flexible and Patient**

    Life is unpredictable, and flexibility is critical to maintaining a long-term routine. Allow yourself to adapt your schedule as needed and be patient with setbacks. Sustainable habits are built over time, not overnight.

Achieving Peace of Mind Through Healthy Living in Life, Business, and Sports is Closely Tied to a Healthy Lifestyle.

Maintaining physical health through regular exercise, proper nutrition, and adequate sleep can significantly enhance focus and productivity in the fast-paced business world. This holistic approach reduces stress and fosters resilience when facing challenges or setbacks. Similarly, prioritizing physical fitness and mental well-being in sports is essential for peak performance. Athletes who embrace balanced diets and engage in mindfulness practices often report improved concentration and reduced anxiety levels, translating to better results on the field. By integrating wellness habits into their routines, individuals in both realms cultivate a sense of balance and tranquility, allowing them to navigate pressures with greater ease and confidence. Ultimately, a commitment to healthy living is the foundation for sustained success and emotional equilibrium in life and work.

Incorporating healthy living principles into daily routines can significantly impact success across various areas of life. By prioritizing health, individuals can unlock their full potential, whether they're at home, in the office, or on the field.

Chapter 19

Listening to Others' Perspective

"Listening is an art that requires attention over talent, spirit over ego, others over self." — **Dean Jackson**

Author Dean Jackson suggests that true listening involves prioritizing others, which is essential for success in any endeavor.

Listening to others' perspectives is not just an exercise in empathy; it's a powerful tool for broadening your understanding and unlocking new ideas. In summary, actively listening not only enriches your own experiences but also contributes to the success of those around you.

Here are Some Key Benefits:

1. **Enhanced Understanding**

- **Life**: Listening to different viewpoints helps you understand diverse experiences and emotions, fostering empathy.
- **Business**: Understanding client or team feedback can lead to better decision-making and innovation.
- **Sports**: Coaches and athletes benefit from understanding each other's strategies and motivations.

2. **Improved Relationships**

- **Life**: Good listening strengthens personal relationships and builds trust.
- **Business**: Active listening promotes collaboration and reduces conflicts within teams.

- **Sports**: It enhances team dynamics, leading to better performance on the field.

3. Informed Decision-Making

- **Life**: Gaining insights from others can lead to more thoughtful life choices.
- **Business**: Listening to market trends and employee suggestions can inform strategic planning.
- **Sports**: Understanding opponents' tactics can lead to more effective game strategies.

4. Increased Adaptability

- **Life**: Being open to others' ideas can help you adapt to new situations and challenges.
- **Business**: Flexibility in responding to feedback can lead to improved products and services.
- **Sports**: Adaptation to different playing styles can enhance team performance.

5. Personal Growth

- **Life**: Engaging with diverse perspectives encourages self-reflection and growth.
- **Business**: Learning from peers and mentors can accelerate professional development.
- **Sports**: Athletes can refine their skills by incorporating feedback from coaches and teammates.

Strategies to Help You Effectively Gather and Consider Differing Perspectives

1. **Diversify Your Network**

   Surround yourself with people from various backgrounds, cultures, and industries. Attend networking events, join diverse groups or forums, and participate in community activities that attract many participants. The more diverse your network, the broader the perspectives you'll encounter.

2. **Engage in Active Listening**

   When conversing with others, practice active listening, which means fully concentrating on what is being said rather than just passively hearing the message. Ask questions to clarify and deepen your understanding, which will help you absorb the full context of their viewpoints.

3. **Seek Constructive Debate**

   Participate in or initiate discussions where differing viewpoints are encouraged. Workplaces, educational settings, and even social media platforms can be suitable venues for engaging in debates that challenge your thinking and expose you to new ideas.

4. **Read Widely and Variedly**

   Expose yourself to a wide range of materials that reflect different perspectives, which include books, newspapers, magazines, and blogs from various parts of the world, across the political spectrum, and from other fields of study.

5. **Use the Devil's Advocate Approach**

   When evaluating a situation or decision, deliberately take the opposite stance from what you believe. This is often referred to as 'the Devil's Advocate Approach '. By doing so, you can help uncover any cognitive biases you might have and present new insights into the issue at hand.

6. **Travel and Experience Different Cultures**

   Travel to different parts of the world or immerse yourself in other cultural experiences locally. Exposure to different ways of life and problem-solving can dramatically broaden your perspective.

7. **Attend Workshops and Seminars**

   Look for learning opportunities that are outside of your expertise or comfort zone. Workshops, seminars, and guest lectures can provide insights into other fields' operations and thinking.

8. **Solicit Feedback Regularly**

   Ask for feedback on your ideas and work from a wide range of people. This could be through formal work processes or informal feedback from peers and mentors. When asking for feedback, it's important to be specific about what you want to learn and to create a safe space for honest responses. Understanding how others perceive your work can offer new perspectives and suggestions for improvement.

9. **Reflect on Your Biases**

   Regularly reflect on your biases and where they might be limiting your understanding. Self-awareness is crucial in recognizing when you might dismiss other viewpoints too quickly.

10. **Use Social Media Intelligently**

   Follow various thinkers and leaders who come from different backgrounds or hold different opinions from your own. Engaging with diverse content on social media can be a convenient way to access a variety of perspectives.

By employing these strategies, you will enrich your understanding of the world and equip yourself to make more informed, well-rounded decisions in all aspects of life.

Achieving Peace of Mind in Life, Business, and Sports Can Significantly Benefit from Actively Listening to Others' Perspectives

When individuals take the time to hear and understand different viewpoints, it fosters empathy and encourages open communication. In the workplace, leaders who consider their team members' ideas and concerns create an inclusive environment where everyone feels valued, promoting collaboration and reducing conflict. Similarly, in sports, teammates sharing their experiences and strategies can enhance team cohesion, improving performance and morale. By embracing diverse perspectives, individuals not only cultivate a richer understanding of their surroundings but also find a sense of peace that comes from knowing they are part of a supportive community. This practice of listening and learning ultimately paves the way for greater personal and professional harmony.

Chapter 20

Problem Solving – The Key to the NEXT Level

Elon Musk (Tesla CEO) demanded to know why his team was not producing 5,000 new cars a week. He brought in the managers, and they said the problem was the steel supplier was not getting the materials to them fast enough. Elon immediately fired the entire staff! Why, because they did not solve the problem. The next team he brought in produced 5,000 cars per week.

We have all heard this many times: How did so and so get that job, position scholarship or drafted ahead of me - I'm more talented! If there are two people with equal talent, which one will advance to the next level? *The person who can solve problems, and solve them quickly, will ultimately move on to the next level.*

Problem Solving, Task, or Critical Decision Plan

When faced with a critical decision or complex problem, having a structured approach can make all the difference. Here's a simple yet effective plan to guide you through the process:

Step 1: **Determine How Much Time You Have to Make a Decision**

- Minutes, days, or months

Step 2**: Define the Best-Case Scenario**

- **Visualize Success**: Imagine the ideal outcome of your decision or solution.

Step 3: **Consider the Worst-Case Scenario**

- **Risk Assessment**: Identify potential downsides and risks associated with the decision. Decide if the worst-case scenario is acceptable and manageable.

Step 4: **Seek Input from Involved Parties**

- **Collaboration and Communication**: Make sure to reach out to key stakeholders or people involved in the process.

- **Gather Perspectives**: Understand their feelings, opinions, and any additional insights they may offer.

- **Foster Buy-In**: Collaborate to ensure that everyone is aligned and engaged with the decision or solution.

Step 5: **Weigh the Positives and Negatives** (If you have a few days to make the decision)

Two-Column Analysis:

- **Positives**: List all the advantages, benefits, and opportunities associated with the decision or problem-solving approach.

- **Negatives**: List the challenges, risks, and potential downsides.

- **Balanced Perspective**: This exercise will help you gain clarity by providing a balanced perspective on the decision.

Step 6: **Make the Decision**

- **Evaluate Options**: With all the information gathered, evaluate your options considering both the best- and worst-case scenarios.

- **Confident Choice**: Make an informed and confident decision based on your analysis and the input of others.

- **Action Plan**: Stick to the plan

By following these steps, you can approach any problem or decision with clarity and confidence. Remember, the goal is to make well-informed choices that align with both your goals and the realities of the situation.

Applying Problem-Solving in Different Areas

For Entrepreneurs

Entrepreneurs often face unique challenges, from securing funding to managing teams. Using peaceful problem-solving techniques can help you maintain a clear mind, make better decisions, and foster a positive work environment. A person will be better equipped to lead your business to success by staying calm and collected.

For Athletes

Athletes are no strangers to pressure and competition. Peaceful problem-solving can help you stay focused and composed, whether dealing with a formidable opponent or recovering from an injury. By defining your challenges clearly and brainstorming solutions, you can develop a winning strategy that keeps you at the top of your game.

For Life Coaches

Life coaches play a crucial role in helping clients overcome personal and professional challenges. Mastering peaceful problem-solving can provide more practical guidance and support. Teaching your clients these techniques can empower them to handle their problems confidently and gracefully.

Problem-solving skills are versatile and can be effective across various scenarios in both professional and personal contexts.

Here are a few practical examples illustrating how problem-solving skills can be effectively utilized in various contexts:

Professional Contexts

1. **Project Management:** For instance, if a project is running behind schedule, you can break down the project into smaller components, identify bottlenecks, and allocate additional resources or adjust timelines accordingly. Use tools like Gantt charts to assess progress and reallocate priorities visually.

- **Scenario:** A project is running behind schedule.

- **Problem-Solving:** Break down the project into smaller components, identify bottlenecks, and allocate additional resources or adjust timelines accordingly. Use tools like Gantt charts to assess progress and reallocate priorities visually.

2. **Customer Service:**

- **Scenario:** A customer is dissatisfied with a product or service.

- **Problem-Solving:** Listen actively to the customer's complaint, identify the core issue, and explore various solutions, such as a replacement, refund, or additional services that could rectify the problem. Implement feedback systems to prevent future occurrences.

3. **IT and Software Development:**

- **Scenario:** Software has recurrent bugs affecting user experience.

- **Problem-Solving:** Use debugging tools to isolate the codes causing the problem, then consult with team members to brainstorm fixes, and apply patches. Implement rigorous testing phases to capture potential issues before release.

Personal Context

1. **Home Budgeting:**

   - **Scenario:** Monthly expenses consistently exceed income.

   - **Problem-Solving:** Analyze spending patterns, identify non-essential expenditures to be reduced, and create a revised budget. Use budgeting apps to track spending and set alerts for when you're approaching your limits.

2. **Relationship Management:**

   - **Scenario:** Frequent misunderstandings with a partner.

   - **Problem-Solving:** Establish a dedicated time to communicate grievances without interruptions, actively listen to each other's concerns, and work together to devise mutually acceptable solutions. Consider relationship counseling if needed.

3. **Health and Fitness:**

   - **Scenario:** Need help maintaining a regular exercise schedule.

   - **Problem-Solving:** Identify specific barriers (time constraints, lack of motivation), explore potential solutions (scheduling workouts at more convenient times, finding an exercise buddy), and set small, measurable goals to stay motivated.

Educational Context

Learning New Skills:
- **Scenario:** Struggling with learning a new language.

- **Problem-Solving:** Identify specific challenges (vocabulary, grammar, pronunciation), use targeted resources (language apps, flashcards, language exchange meetups), and adjust learning methods based on what proves most effective.

Community Involvement

Neighborhood Issues:

- **Scenario:** Increase in local crime rates.

- **Problem-Solving:** To enhance safety, organize a neighborhood watch group, collaborate with local law enforcement for safety workshops, and implement community-driven initiatives like better street lighting.

Achieving Peace of Mind Through Effective Problem Solving in Life, Business, and Sports

Navigating the complexities of life, business, and sports can often feel overwhelming, but cultivating practical problem-solving skills can lead to a profound sense of peace and confidence.

In life, approaching challenges with a solution-oriented mindset allows parents to model resilience and adaptability for their children, showcasing that setbacks are merely stepping stones to success.

In business, fostering a culture of open communication and collaboration can empower teams to tackle obstacles collectively, reducing stress and enhancing productivity.

Lastly, teaching children to analyze game situations and develop strategic responses in sports nurtures critical thinking. It improves their ability to cope with pressure. By integrating these problem-solving approaches across various domains, parents can enhance their peace of mind and cultivate a nurturing environment that encourages their children to embrace challenges with courage and optimism.

Chapter 21

Embrace Competition

Health expert David Leonardi affirms that engaging in competition fosters personal growth and betterment through self-analysis and effort.

"Don't limit your challenges. Challenge your limits." - **David Leonardi**

This quote encourages embracing competition by pushing one's boundaries and striving beyond perceived limitations.

Competition often gets a bad rap, portrayed as a cutthroat battle where only the strongest survive. But what if we told you that competition isn't about defeating others but improving yourself? It fosters innovation, encourages growth, and ultimately leads to a higher standard of excellence. Whether you're an entrepreneur, an innovator, an athlete, or a student, here's why you should be excited about competition.

Competition in Life Drives Innovation

The Tech Giants' Rivalry

Take the tech industry, for example. The rivalry between Apple and Microsoft is legendary. This competitive spirit has led both companies to push the boundaries of what's possible, resulting in significant advancements in computing. From user-friendly interfaces to robust software, consumers have benefited immensely from the innovations spurred by this rivalry.

The Space Race

Remember the Space Race? The intense competition between the United States and the Soviet Union in the 1950s and 1960s sparked a wave of scientific and technological advancements. This race to space led to the first human moon landing in 1969 and accelerated developments in satellite technology, telecommunications, and even everyday items like microwaves and GPS.

Competition in Sports Encourages Personal Growth

Serena vs. Venus Williams

In sports, the intense rivalry between tennis greats Serena Williams and Venus Williams has elevated the women's game and inspired a new generation of athletes. Their competition has pushed each sister to refine her skills, stay fit, and strive for excellence. This personal growth has resulted in numerous Grand Slam titles and enduring legacies for both players.

The Darwin Awards

Even in the realm of sustainability, competition can inspire positive change. The annual "Darwin Awards" celebrate innovative solutions to environmental challenges. This friendly competition encourages individuals and communities to adopt eco-friendly practices, benefiting the planet and future generations.

Competition in Business Leads to Better Products and Services

The Cola Wars

Consider the "cola wars" between Coca-Cola and Pepsi. This long-standing rivalry has led to continuous product innovation and creative marketing strategies. Both companies constantly try to outdo each other with new flavors, healthier options, and clever advertising campaigns. The result? Consumers get a wider variety of high-quality products to choose from. Similarly, the competition between Samsung and Apple has led to significant advancements in smartphone technology, with each company striving to out-innovate the other in terms of design, features, and user experience.

How to Embrace Competition

1. **Shift Your Mindset**: See competition as a learning opportunity. What can you learn from your competitors that can help you improve?

2. **Focus on Growth**: Use competition as a catalyst for personal and professional development. Aim to be better than you were yesterday.

3. **Innovate Continuously**: Don't rest on your laurels. Always look for ways to innovate and offer your audience or customers more value.

4. **Build Resilience**: Competition can be challenging, but it builds resilience. Learn to bounce back from setbacks more muscularly and determinedly.

5. **Collaborate and Network**: Sometimes, your competitors can become your best allies. Look for opportunities to collaborate and benefit mutually.

Competition is a Driving Force

Competition is a powerful force that drives innovation, encourages personal growth, and leads to better products and services. It's not about defeating others, but pushing yourself to be your best. So, whether you're an entrepreneur looking to innovate, an athlete striving for excellence, or a student aiming to improve, remember that competition can be your greatest ally. Embracing competition not only leads to professional success but also contributes to your personal fulfillment and peace of mind.

Fostering a competitive mindset can be a powerful tool for personal growth, enabling individuals to maximize their potential and achieve their goals.

Here are Several Strategies to Help Cultivate Such a Mindset:

1. **Set Clear and Challenging Goals**

    Begin by setting specific, measurable, and challenging goals. These goals should stretch your abilities and motivate you to push beyond your comfort zone. By aiming high, you encourage yourself to develop the skills and strategies needed to succeed.

2. **Embrace Learning and Self-Improvement**

    Adopt a mindset focused on continuous learning and self-improvement. View every experience, whether a success or failure, as an opportunity to learn. Invest time in acquiring new skills, attending workshops, reading, and seeking feedback to enhance your capabilities.

3. **Analyze Competitors' Strengths**

    Learn from others who excel in your field. Analyze what makes them successful, study their strategies, and adapt their best practices to fit your unique context. Thus, something other than copying them directly, but learning from, and deriving inspiration from their achievements.

4. **Benchmark Performance**

    Regularly compare your performance against your past achievements and the standards your peers or leaders in your field set. This benchmarking process helps identify performance gaps and areas for improvement.

5. **Cultivate Resilience**

    Developing resilience is critical to maintaining a competitive edge. Learn to handle criticism constructively and bounce back from setbacks with a positive attitude. Resilience will empower you to face challenges head-on and stay committed to your goals despite obstacles. It's this resilience that will make you a formidable competitor, ready to take on any challenge that comes your way.

6. **Seek Constructive Competition**

   Engage in healthy competition, such as participating in contests, challenges, or games relevant to your goals. These activities can simulate stress and pressure similar to real-life scenarios, helping you sharpen your skills under pressure.

7. **Visualize Success**

   Practice visualization techniques by imagining achieving your goals and overcoming obstacles. This mental rehearsal can boost your confidence and help you mentally prepare for the path to success.

8. **Maintain a Positive Attitude**

   Keep a positive outlook and believe in your ability to succeed. A positive attitude helps you stay energized and motivated, even when facing difficulties.

9. **Stay Informed and Adaptive**

   Keep up with the latest trends and technologies in your field. Being well-informed allows you to adapt to changes quickly and seize opportunities that others might overlook. In a competitive environment, staying informed and adaptive is not just an advantage, it's a necessity. It's what will keep you ahead of the curve and ready to tackle any new challenge that comes your way.

10. **Celebrate Milestones**

    Recognize and celebrate small victories along the way. This will not only boost morale but also reinforce the value of your efforts and keep you motivated to achieve your larger goals.

By integrating these strategies into your daily life, you can foster a competitive mindset that drives personal growth and prepares you to handle the complexities of varied challenges in both personal and professional spheres.

Embracing competition has historically been a key driver behind many significant breakthroughs and innovations across various industries. Here are some notable examples:

1. **Space Exploration**

   SpaceX vs. Traditional Aerospace: The entry of private companies like SpaceX into a government-led space sector has sparked significant innovation and reduced costs in space travel. SpaceX's competitive approach introduced reusable rocket technology with its Falcon series, drastically cutting the cost of space missions and enabling more ambitious projects like Mars colonization plans.

2. **Technology and Consumer Electronics**

   Apple vs. Samsung: Apple and Samsung's rivalry in the smartphone market has led to rapid technological advancements in mobile technology. Each iteration of their devices often includes significant enhancements in processor speed, camera technology, battery life, and display technology, pushing the envelope of what smartphones can do.

3. **Automotive Industry**

   Tesla vs. Major Automakers: Tesla's success in popularizing electric vehicles prompted traditional automakers like Ford, Volkswagen, and General Motors to accelerate their electric vehicle programs. This competition has spurred a wave of innovation in electric vehicle technology, battery efficiency, and charging infrastructure, contributing to the global shift towards sustainable transportation.

4. **Streaming Services**

   Netflix vs. Hulu, Amazon Prime Video, and Others: Netflix's early success in streaming video content prompted fierce competition from other companies like Hulu, Amazon Prime Video, and, more recently, Disney+ and Apple TV+. This competition has expanded viewing options and significantly increased the production and quality of original content, transforming how audiences consume media and entertainment.

5. **E-commerce**

   Amazon vs. Retail Giants: Amazon's rise in the e-commerce sector pushed traditional retail giants like Walmart, Target, and Best Buy to enhance their online presence and service offerings, including faster shipping options, price matching, and improved e-commerce platforms. This competition has benefited consumers through better service, lower prices, and greater convenience.

6. **Pharmaceuticals**

   COVID-19 Vaccine Development: The global urgency to develop a COVID-19 vaccine saw pharmaceutical giants like Pfizer, Moderna, and AstraZeneca in a race against time. The competitive push helped accelerate what would typically be a decade-long process into under a year, demonstrating how competition can drive extraordinary achievements in a short period.

These examples underscore how competition pushes companies to innovate and often leads to broader societal benefits such as increased consumer choice, better products and services, and significant technological and scientific advancements.

Achieving Peace of Mind by Embracing Competition in Life, Business, and Sports

Embracing competition in life, business, and sports can contribute significantly to peace of mind. Rather than viewing rivals as threats, adopt a mindset that sees competition as a catalyst for improvement which can foster resilience and personal growth.

In life, striving against challenges can motivate individuals to set and accomplish personal goals, enhancing self-esteem and satisfaction.

In business, competition drives innovation and efficiency, ensuring that companies continuously improve their services and products, which can lead to greater customer satisfaction and loyalty.

In sports, competing not only hones athletic abilities but also provides valuable lessons in teamwork and perseverance.

By recognizing competition as an opportunity for development rather than a hindrance, individuals can cultivate a more balanced, fulfilling perspective, ultimately gaining a sense of peace and purpose in their endeavors.

Chapter 22

Stay in the Moment

"You can't hold on to what was or worry about what will be. You just have to stay focused on this very moment." — Serena Williams

Serena Williams, a legendary tennis champion, shares her insight that dwelling on the past or worrying about the future can hinder performance, highlighting the necessity of concentrating on the here and now.

In the fast-paced worlds of business and sports, it's easy to get caught up in the rush to succeed. But what if the key to true success—and peace of mind—lies in a more straightforward approach? By focusing on the present moment and taking life one day at a time, one game at a time and one play at a time, you can cultivate a mindset that keeps you grounded and drives long-term success.

Critical Principles for Achieving Peace of Mind

One of the most essential strategies for finding peace of mind is to stay in the moment by avoiding the temptation to worry about future outcomes, such as the score in a game or the success of a business venture. Instead, concentrate on the task at hand. By doing so, you can give your best performance without the burden of future anxieties, experiencing a sense of relief and freedom.

Focus on Fundamentals and the Game Plan

Whether an entrepreneur or an athlete, focusing on the fundamentals and sticking to your game plan is crucial. Instead of getting lost in the bigger picture, zero in on the basics within your control. This approach empowers you to build a strong foundation essential for sustainable success, putting you in the driver's seat of your journey.

Staying in the moment is crucial for success in life, business, and sports. Here are some key points on why this mindset is important:

1. **Enhanced Focus**

    - Staying present allows you to concentrate fully on the task at hand, reducing distractions and improving performance.

2. **Improved Decision-Making**

    - When you're focused on the moment, you're better equipped to make timely and informed decisions without being swayed by past failures or future anxieties.

3. **Increased Resilience**

    - Being mindful helps you cope with setbacks. Instead of dwelling on what went wrong, you can learn from the experience and move forward.

4. **Boosted Creativity**

    - A present mindset encourages open-mindedness and adaptability, fostering innovative thinking and problem-solving.

5. **Strengthened Relationships**

    - In business and personal interactions, being present enhances communication and connection, leading to more meaningful relationships.

6. **Heightened Performance**

    - In sports, athletes who stay in the moment often perform better. They can react instinctively and maintain peak performance without overthinking.

7. **Mental Well-Being**
   - Practicing mindfulness reduces stress and anxiety, promoting overall mental health, which is essential for sustained success.

Success Stories

Numerous success stories highlight the benefits of taking one day at a time and trusting the process. These stories can inspire you, showing that with the right mindset and approach, success is not just a distant dream, but a tangible reality.

Business Success

Consider the story of Sarah, a small business owner overwhelmed by the pressure to scale her business quickly. Instead of stressing over future growth, she focused on refining her product and providing excellent customer service daily. Over time, her business flourished organically, with loyal customers and steady growth.

Sports Achievement

In sports, Michael, a college basketball player, was constantly stressed about winning games. His coach advised him to focus on his daily training and practice sessions rather than the scoreboard. By concentrating on perfecting his skills and following the team's strategy, he became a more confident and influential player, contributing significantly to his team's success.

Practical Tips for Entrepreneurs, Athletes, and Teammates

For Entrepreneurs

1. **Daily Goals**: Break your long-term business goals into daily tasks that are manageable and achievable.

2. Mindfulness: Practice mindfulness techniques to stay focused and present throughout the day.

3. Celebrate Small Wins: Recognize and celebrate small achievements to keep yourself motivated.

For Athletes

1. Training Focus: Concentrate on improving one aspect of your game each day.

2. Game Preparation: Stick to your pre-game routines and trust the preparation you've put in.

3. Stay Positive: Maintain a positive attitude, even when things aren't going as planned.

For Teammates

1. Support Each Other: Encourage your teammates to focus on the present moment and trust the team's strategy.

2. Communicate Effectively: Keep open lines of communication to ensure everyone is aligned and focused.

3. Trust the Process: Believe in the collective effort and understand that success is gradual.

Staying in the Moment for Success in Life, Business, and Sports doesn't have to be a complex endeavor. By staying in the moment, focusing on the fundamentals, and taking one day at a time, you can lay the groundwork for lasting achievements.

Ready to Take the First Step Towards a More Focused and Peaceful Mindset?

Remember, small, consistent actions lead to significant results. Start today, and watch how your approach transforms your life, business, and sports performance.

Chapter 23

Strive to be the BEST: Locally, Nationally, and Globally

"Champions keep playing until they get it right." — **Billie Jean King**

Billie Jean King, a pioneering tennis champion, attributes success to continuously striving to be the best you can be, even under stress, is essential to mastering one's craft and achieving excellence.

They strive to be the best—local, national, or global—requiring a commitment to excellence and a proactive approach to growth and innovation. This ambition propels individuals and organizations to meet and exceed the standards set by their peers and competitors.

Striving to be the best in various aspects of life—locally, nationally, and globally—involves a multifaceted approach. Here are some key areas to focus on:

1. Personal Development

- **Continuous Learning:** Always seek knowledge through books, courses, and experiences.
- **Goal Setting:** Set clear, achievable goals and regularly assess your progress.
- **Self-Discipline:** Cultivate habits that promote consistency and perseverance.

2. Business Excellence

- **Innovation:** Stay ahead of the game by embracing new ideas and technologies.

- **Customer Focus:** Understand and anticipate customer needs to enhance satisfaction and loyalty.

- **Networking:** Build relationships with industry leaders and peers to exchange knowledge and opportunities.

3. Sports Achievement

- **Training Regimen:** Commit to a rigorous training schedule that develops both physical and mental strength.

- **Teamwork:** Collaborate effectively with teammates, fostering a supportive environment.

- **Mindset:** Develop resilience and a positive attitude to overcome challenges and setbacks.

4. Community Engagement

- **Volunteering:** Give back to your local community through service and support.

- **Mentorship:** Share your knowledge and personal experiences with others to help them grow.

- **Sustainability:** Advocate for practices that will help protect the environment for future generations.

5. Global Perspective

- **Cultural Awareness:** Understand and respect diverse cultures in both business and personal interactions.

- **Global Challenges:** Stay informed about global issues and consider how your actions can contribute to solutions.

- **Collaboration:** Work with international partners to share ideas and resources for mutual benefit.

Being the best locally involves deeply understanding and catering to community needs, building a solid reputation grounded in trust and quality.

Nationally, the scope widens, and the focus shifts to setting benchmarks that distinguish one from the larger domestic market through superior service, product quality, and innovation.

On a global level, the challenge is to embrace and adapt to international standards, cultural diversity, and competitive dynamics, all while pushing the boundaries of what's possible.

Achieving such heights demands a relentless pursuit of knowledge, openness to new ideas, and a willingness to adapt and evolve. Success at these levels elevates one's status and often sets new paradigms in excellence, inspiring others and driving sectors forward.

Organizations that successfully thrive in diverse markets often do so by mastering a combination of strategic, operational, and cultural factors. These factors enable them to adapt and excel, regardless of the geographical or economic context.

Here are some key elements that contribute to their success:

1. Adaptability

Successful organizations are highly adaptable, capable of adjusting their strategies, products, and services to meet the changing demands and unique challenges of different markets. This flexibility is a crucial factor that allows them to respond quickly to new opportunities or threats, ensuring they remain competitive and relevant.

2. Understanding Local Markets

Deep knowledge of local markets is crucial, as is understanding cultural nuances, consumer behavior, local regulations, and market dynamics. Organizations that invest in local market research can tailor their offerings to satisfy local preferences better and comply with local standards, giving them a competitive edge.

3. Robust Global Strategy

While local adaptation is crucial, thriving organizations maintain a robust global strategy. This strategy ensures that their local actions contribute towards their international goals, creating a coherent brand identity and unified business objectives across all markets.

4. Innovation

Innovation is a key strategy that helps organizations stay ahead in competitive markets. Innovative practices enable organizations to capture and create unique value propositions across diverse markets, whether through product development, technology adoption, or new business models.

5. Talent Management

Attracting, developing, and retaining talent is essential for an organization's success. Cultivating a diverse workforce with local and international expertise enriches the organization's understanding and operational capability in various markets.

6. Technological Integration

Leveraging technology can dramatically enhance an organization's efficiency and scalability. From improving supply chain logistics to offering digital customer experiences, technology enables businesses to operate seamlessly across borders.

7. Sustainable Practices

Commitment to sustainability resonates well across global markets, particularly as consumers and regulations increasingly favor environmentally and socially responsible companies. Sustainable practices not only help in building a positive brand image but also ensure long-term viability.

8. Effective Communication

Communication that transcends cultural and linguistic barriers is fundamental. Organizations that invest in effective communication strategies can better align and inspire their global teams while engaging effectively with customers in diverse regions.

9. Strategic Partnerships

Forming alliances with local or regional businesses can provide valuable insights and entry points into a new market. These partnerships can mitigate risks associated with market entry and provide synergistic benefits that might not be achievable alone.

10. Customer-Centric Approach

Keeping the customer at the center of decision-making and focusing on delivering superior value and service helps build loyalty and positive word of mouth, which are crucial for success in any market or field.

Organizations that excel in these areas can establish their presence across different markets and sustain growth and profitability in the long term, effectively turning global diversity into a strategic advantage.

Finding Peace of Mind with Success While Striving to be the BEST in Life, Business and Sports

Regardless of our goals and pursuits, it is essential to remember that true success comes from within. By focusing on the present moment, setting achievable daily goals, and trusting in the team's strategy, we can cultivate a sense of peace and fulfillment in our journey toward achieving our ultimate objective.

Chapter 24

Building the Best TEAM

"We want to build the DREAM TEAM. Here are the two questions all our managers have to ask themselves about each team member:

- *If the employee wants to leave the company, will you fight to keep them?*

- *If the employee leaves, would you hire them again?*

If you answer no to both questions, you must fire them." - Ted Sarandos, Netflix CEO

A truly remarkable team can achieve what an individual alone never could. Whether you're an entrepreneur, a coach, or a team leader, the principles of building a high-performing team remain the same. Let's explore these principles and examine examples of successful teams in life, business, and sports.

Critical Principles for Building the Best Team

1. Intelligence

Selecting team members with high intelligence is crucial. Intelligence isn't just about having book smarts; it's about understanding complex problems and coming up with innovative solutions. Intelligent team members can adapt quickly to changes, learn new skills efficiently, and think strategically.

2. Drive

The drive is the relentless pursuit of goals. A team with driven individuals who are self-motivated and self - disciplined to push through obstacles, meet deadlines, and exceed expectations. Driven team members inspire others, creating a culture of ambition and high performance.

3. Motivation

Motivation is the inner fire that fuels persistence and resilience. A motivated team is enthusiastic, energetic, and committed to its work. It finds meaning in its tasks and is willing to go the extra mile to achieve shared goals.

4. Problem-Solving Ability

The ability to solve problems effectively is a must for any team. When challenges arise, team members with strong problem-solving skills can analyze the situation, brainstorm solutions, and implement strategies swiftly, leading to quicker resolutions and less disruption in achieving objectives.

Examples of Successful Teams

Life

In life, one of the most impactful teams you can build is your support network. Your network might include family, friends, mentors, and advisors. For instance, Apple co-founder Steve Jobs often credited his success not just to his abilities but to the supportive network he had around him, including his close friend and colleague Steve Wozniak.

Business

In business, successful teams often consist of diverse skills and perspectives. Take Google's founding team, for example. Both knowledgeable and driven, Larry Page and Sergey Brin complemented each other's strengths and weaknesses. They recruited talented engineers and leaders who were motivated and could solve complex problems, leading to the creation of one of the most influential companies in the world.

Sports

In sports, legendary teams like the Chicago Bulls of the 1990s testify to the power of selecting the right people. Michael Jordan, Scottie Pippen, and Dennis Rodman were exceptional athletes and brilliant players who understood the game deeply. Their drive, motivation, and problem-solving abilities on the court led them to multiple NBA championships.

Build Your Dream Team

To build your dream team, you must be strategic and intentional about your choices. Here's a step-by-step guide:

1. Identify Your Needs

Determine what specific skills and attributes you need to achieve your goals and target suitable candidates.

2. Look for Complementary Skills

A well-rounded team has multiple members with diverse skills that complement each other. Look for individuals who can fill gaps and bring unique perspectives.

3. Assess Drive and Motivation

During the selection process, assess candidates for their drive and motivation. Ask questions about their long-term goals, what drives them, and how they stay motivated.

4. Test Problem-Solving Abilities

During interviews, give candidates real-world problems to solve. This will help you gauge their problem-solving abilities and approach to challenges.

5. Foster a Positive Culture

Create an environment that supports growth, collaboration, and mutual respect. A positive culture will attract and retain top talent.

Building a Cohesive Team That Will Effectively Leverage Diverse Perspectives and Skills Fosters Innovation and Achieves Superior Results

Here's a detailed approach to creating such a team:

1. Diverse Recruitment

Start by ensuring your recruitment strategies are designed to attract diverse candidates. This includes diversity in terms of race, gender, and ethnicity, as well as skills, experiences, and backgrounds. Utilize varied recruitment channels and practices to reach a broader audience, fostering an inclusive and open-minded team culture.

2. Inclusive Culture

Cultivate an inclusive workplace culture where all team members feel valued and respected. It involves promoting open communication, respect for different viewpoints, and an organizational commitment to equality. Training sessions on diversity, inclusion, and cultural competency can deepen understanding and reduce biases.

3. Role and Responsibility Clarity

Clearly define roles and responsibilities within the team to ensure that everyone understands their tasks and how their work contributes to the organization's overall objectives. This clarity helps minimize conflicts and overlaps, allowing for more efficient and organized team dynamics.

4. Strength-Based Assignments

Identify and utilize each team member's unique strengths. Assign tasks based on individual skills and experiences to optimize performance. This will enhance productivity and boost morale and job satisfaction as employees feel their specific skills are being recognized and utilized.

5. Effective Communication

Establish strong communication channels and norms. Encourage regular team meetings, updates, and open dialogues where team members can share ideas and feedback. Effective communication is essential for aligning team efforts and integrating diverse perspectives into actionable strategies.

6. Conflict Resolution Mechanisms

Develop and maintain effective conflict resolution mechanisms. Disagreements are inevitable in diverse teams, but how they are managed determines the team's resilience and cohesiveness. Training team members in conflict resolution and problem-solving skills can help maintain harmony and collaboration.

7. Collaborative Decision-Making

Involve team members in decision-making processes. Tapping into a wide range of ideas and insights fosters a sense of ownership and commitment to the team's goals. Use techniques like brainstorming sessions and consensus-building to encourage active participation.

8. Professional Development

Invest in team members' continuous professional development. Offer training programs, workshops, and courses that enhance individual skills and benefit the team as a whole. Encourage cross-training and mentoring within the team to share knowledge and skills.

9. Celebrating Diversity

Recognize and celebrate team members' diverse backgrounds and achievements through cultural awareness events. These team-building activities highlight diversity and foster a culture of appreciation and respect.

10. Regular Feedback and Assessment

Implement a feedback system where team members can give and receive constructive feedback. Regular performance assessments at individual and team levels help identify areas for improvement and strategies for better leveraging the team's diverse capabilities.

By focusing on these strategies, organizations can build teams that are not only diverse but also cohesive and effective, turning diversity into a competitive advantage and driving the organization toward its goals. Team-building activities are essential tools for enhancing collaboration and leveraging the diverse strengths of team members. Practical activities can range from problem-solving challenges to more socially focused events, each designed to highlight and utilize a team's varied skills and perspectives. Here are several examples of successful team-building activities that can help achieve these goals:

11. Skills-Based Workshops

Organize workshops where team members can teach each other specific skills or knowledge areas where they excel. For example, a team member fluent in a second language could give an introductory language lesson, or someone with advanced Excel skills could offer a spreadsheet management workshop. Exercising this route will help in skill sharing and recognizing and appreciating the diverse talents within the team.

12. Role Swapping

Allow team members to temporarily swap roles or shadow someone in a different role within the organization. This activity can foster empathy and deeper understanding among team members, highlighting the unique challenges and skills required in different positions.

13. Escape Rooms

Escape rooms are excellent for cultivating teamwork and problem-solving skills. They require team members to work together under time pressure, utilizing different thinking styles and perspectives to solve puzzles and escape the room. This can be particularly effective in recognizing and valuing different approaches to problem-solving.

14. Hackathons

Conduct a hackathon where team members can propose and develop solutions to existing problems within the company or start entirely new projects. This activity encourages innovation and allows individuals to use their unique skills creatively and collaboratively.

15. Cooking Challenges

Organize cooking challenges or potluck events where team members can prepare dishes from their cultural backgrounds. Food is a universal language and can be a delightful and inclusive way to learn about and celebrate the diverse cultures within your team.

16. Outdoor Team Sports

Sporting events like soccer, basketball, or even something less conventional like ultimate Frisbee or kickball can help build team spirit. Sports require coordination, communication, and strategy, allowing individuals to showcase leadership and teamwork skills.

17. Community Service Projects

Engage the team in a community service project that aligns with the company's CSR values. Whether building homes, cleaning up local parks, or volunteering at food banks, working together for the common good can strengthen bonds and show the impact of collective effort.

18. Innovation Tournaments

Host an innovation tournament where teams compete to develop a new product idea or solve a company challenge. This will encourage creative thinking and draw on team members' diverse backgrounds and skills, from creativity and technical skills to strategic planning.

19. Professional Development Groups

Create small groups focused on specific areas of professional development, such as public speaking, project management, or digital marketing. These groups can meet regularly to share resources, discuss ideas, and support each other's growth, leveraging the unique expertise of each group member.

20. Virtual Reality (VR) Team-Building

For teams that include remote members, VR platforms can offer a unique space for collaborative and interactive experiences that simulate a physical presence. Activities might involve collaborative puzzles or team adventures in a virtual world, accessible to everyone regardless of location.

These activities not only help build a cohesive team but also ensure that all team members' unique strengths and perspectives are acknowledged and utilized, thereby enhancing team performance and job satisfaction.

One of the toughest decisions a CEO, Coach or Entrepreneur will make is "Should I fire an employee or spend the time and resources to develop an employee who is not hitting the goals you projected".

Here are examples of ineffective leadership:

1. Indecisiveness

When a leader is confronted with an important decision and they analyze repeatedly, delaying action. Don't waste everyone's time.

2. Problem Solving Inability

This is the key to getting to the next level. If you can't do this quickly or at all the family, company, or team is doomed for failure.

3. No Clarity with Priorities

The leader issues 10-20 tasks and says ALL of these are important!

4. The Leader Speaks in Technical Language Instead of Inspiring

He leaves them bored and no clear path.

5. Constantly Criticizing with No Positive Reinforcement

One single mistake by an individual should not haunt them forever. Give the individual a chance to learn from their mistake.

6. Never Communicating with a Clear Vision

Therefore, the team is left with no clarity for a path to success.

7. Inaccessibility

Confine yourself to an office all day instead of getting out in the hallways, job sites or on the field with the team.

8. Exercising "Power" is Not True Leadership

True leadership is when individuals follow when they would otherwise have the freedom to *not* follow.

Achieve Peace of Mind by Building the Best Team in Life, Business, and Sports

Constructing an effective team is critical to achieving peace of mind, whether in personal relationships, professional settings, or sporting activities. A strong team allows you to share burdens, celebrate successes, and navigate challenges together.

In life, surrounding yourself with supportive friends and family who encourage personal growth fosters a sense of security and belonging. In business, a well-assembled team mitigates stress and enhances productivity, leading to more incredible innovation and success.

Likewise, having the right teammates can transform the experience in sports, creating camaraderie while pursuing common goals. By investing time and effort into building a team that aligns with your values and aspirations, you enhance your journey and create a solid foundation for peace of mind in all areas of your life.

Building the best team is about more than just assembling a group of talented individuals. It's about choosing people who are intelligent, driven, motivated, and excellent problem solvers. Applying these principles allows you to create a team that excels in life, business, or sports.

Ready to Build Your Dream Team?

Start by identifying the key attributes you need and seek out individuals who embody these qualities. With the right team, there's no limit to what you can achieve.

Chapter 25

Handling Pressure Situations

"Pressure is something you feel when you don't know what you're doing." — **Chuck Noll**

Chuck Noll, renowned NFL coach, posits that confidence and preparedness mitigate pressure. This insight suggests that developing skill and knowledge can transform potentially stressful situations into controlled environments.

Mastering Pressure Management in Life, Business, and Sports

Pressure is an inevitable part of life, whether you're navigating personal challenges, steering a business to success, or competing in high-stakes sports. However, knowing how to handle pressure effectively can bring a sense of relief and make all the difference between achieving your goals and falling short. Here's how you can manage pressure across these critical areas.

Handling Pressure

Everyday life can present numerous pressure-filled situations, from managing family responsibilities to making important personal decisions. Here are some techniques to help you stay focused and effective:

- **Stay Focused and Execute the Plan**: This is where your power lies. Create a Plan: Outline the steps needed to achieve your goal. Break down larger tasks into smaller, more manageable parts.

- **Create a Plan**: Outline the steps needed to achieve your goal. Break down larger tasks into smaller, more manageable parts.

- **Prioritize Tasks**: Determine which tasks are most critical and tackle them first.

- **Stay Organized**: Use calendars, to-do lists, and reminders to keep track of your responsibilities.

- **Practice Mindfulness**: Engage in mindfulness activities like meditation or deep-breathing exercises to keep your mind calm and focused.

Visualize Success

- **Positive Visualization**: Picture yourself completing tasks and overcoming challenges, which can boost your confidence and reduce anxiety.

- **Affirmations**: Repeat positive affirmations to reinforce your ability to handle pressure effectively.

Life

Consider a mother juggling a full-time job while raising two kids. She creates a weekly schedule, prioritizes family time, and uses positive visualization to maintain her focus and composure. By planning and staying organized, she balances her responsibilities without feeling overwhelmed.

Managing Pressure in Business

In the business world, pressure comes in many forms, such as meeting deadlines, achieving targets, or handling client expectations. Effective pressure management is crucial for success.

Plan and Finish the Final Details

- **Strategic Planning**: Develop long-term and short-term plans that align with your business goals. Anticipate potential obstacles and prepare contingency plans.

- **Attention to Detail**: Ensure all aspects of a project are thoroughly completed. Double-check work to maintain high quality and avoid last-minute issues.

Stay Focused on Execution

- **Delegate Wisely**: Assign tasks to team members based on their strengths and expertise.

- **Monitor Progress**: Regularly review project milestones and adjust plans as needed.

- **Communication**: Maintain clear and open communication with your team to ensure everyone is aligned and informed.

Business

Running a residential construction company involves managing multiple moving parts and meeting client expectations. A construction manager can deliver high-quality projects on time, even under pressure, by planning ahead, delegating tasks effectively, and meticulously handling all details.

Sports

Athletes often face intense pressure, whether taking the final shot in a game or competing in a major tournament. Here's how to manage pressure and perform at your best.

Visualize Making the Shot

- **Mental Rehearsal**: Visualize successfully executing your sport's key moves or plays, which will build muscle memory and confidence.

- **Focus on the Process**: Concentrate on the steps needed to perform well rather than the outcome, reducing anxiety and keeping you grounded.

Stay Focused on Execution

- **Breathing Techniques**: Practice controlled breathing to calm your nerves and improve focus.

- **Pre-Performance Routine**: Develop a consistent routine before competitions to mentally and physically prepare yourself.

Imagine a basketball player taking the last shot for a big victory. By visualizing the ball going through the hoop and focusing on their shooting technique, they can block out distractions and confidently execute the shot.

Pressure is a part of life, and some say a little pressure on you now and then is a good thing, but it doesn't have to overwhelm you. You can effectively manage pressure in any situation by staying focused, planning ahead, and visualizing success. Whether navigating life's challenges, leading a business, or competing in sports, these techniques will help you stay calm, focused, and poised for success.

Keys to Success

Limit Distractions

Create an environment where distractions are minimized to maintain clarity of thought and purpose. The pressure and distractions increase significantly in an environment at a large company or a game with a large crowd. Here are some critical thoughts to remember during these pressure-packed situations:

1. Stick to the game plan.

2. Block out the thought: We will lose if I don't close this job or make this shot. Block out the pressure of thinking everything you do means winning or losing.

3. Stay in the moment and focus on the fundamentals.

4. The elite entrepreneurs and athletes relish these pressure situations.

5. Prepare for these situations in practice or role-play with coworkers.

Embrace a Positive Mindset

- **Reframe Challenges**: View pressure situations as opportunities for growth rather than threats. This shift in perspective not only enhances resilience and motivation but also fills you with optimism about the future.

- **Affirmations**: Use positive affirmations to reinforce your ability to manage and thrive under pressure, instilling confidence that guides your actions.

Establish Support Systems

- **Seek Guidance**: Lean on mentors, peers, or coaches who can provide support and encouragement during challenging times. This support system makes you feel more secure and less alone.

- **Collaborate with Teams**: Foster a collaborative atmosphere in business and sports, where team members can share burdens and uplift each other, creating a sense of shared purpose.

Achieving Peace of Mind During Pressure Situations in Life, Business, and Sports

By integrating these practices, individuals can navigate pressure situations more effectively and achieve a tranquil mindset conducive to success. The goal is not to eliminate pressure, but to manage it effectively. Whether navigating life's challenges, leading a business, or competing in sports, these techniques will help you stay calm, focused, and poised for success.

Chapter 26

Commitment and Mental Toughness

"The moment you give up is the moment you let someone else win."
— **Kobe Bryant**

Basketball legend Kobe Bryant motivates us to persist through challenges, reminding us the importance of being mentally tough through hard times

Mental Toughness, sometimes called resilience, is a multifaceted virtue that manifests in various ways across different domains of life, business, and sports. Whether you are an athlete, an entrepreneur, a coach, or a performer, mental Toughness is not just an asset—it's a necessity. In this article, we explore the key themes of resilience and provide you with actionable insights to help strengthen your mental fortitude.

Commitment in relationships plays a significant role in developing mental toughness in various areas of life, including personal relationships, business, and sports. Here's how these concepts interconnect:

Commitment in Relationships

1. **Emotional Resilience**: Commitment fosters emotional stability. In a relationship, facing challenges together builds resilience, which is essential for mental toughness. This emotional support can help individuals cope with stress in other areas of life.

2. **Communication Skills**: Committed relationships often require open communication. Developing these skills can translate to

better negotiation and conflict resolution in business and sports settings.

3. **Long-Term Focus**: Commitment encourages a long-term perspective. In life and business, this mindset helps individuals prioritize goals and maintain motivation through setbacks.

Mental Toughness

1. **Persistence**: Mental toughness involves the ability to persevere through difficulties. People who are committed to their relationships are often more equipped to handle failures and setbacks in other areas, as they have learned the value of persistence.

2. **Adaptability**: Commitment teaches flexibility. In both business and sports, the ability to adapt to changing circumstances is crucial for success. Those who have nurtured their commitment skills can better navigate unexpected challenges.

3. **Self-Discipline**: Commitment requires self-discipline, which is also vital in sports and business. This discipline helps individuals stay focused on their objectives, even when faced with distractions or obstacles.

Application in Business and Sports

1. **Team Dynamics**: In sports, a committed team can outperform a group of talented individuals who lack cohesion. The same applies in business; strong relationships can lead to better teamwork and collaboration.

2. **Goal Alignment**: Commitment in personal relationships can lead to better alignment of goals in business partnerships. Understanding and supporting each other's aspirations fosters a culture of mutual success.

3. **Stress Management**: Both in sports and business, the ability to handle stress is crucial. A strong support system from committed relationships can provide the necessary encouragement and perspective during high-pressure situations.

Commitment in relationships cultivates qualities like resilience, adaptability, and self-discipline, all of which are essential for mental toughness. This interconnectedness reinforces the idea that strong personal connections can enhance performance and well-being in all areas of life, including business and sports. By nurturing commitment, individuals can develop the mental toughness needed to thrive in various challenges they encounter.

Key Themes of Mental Toughness

Grit

Grit is the relentless pursuit of long-term goals. The passion and mental Toughness keep you moving forward, even when the going gets tough. Grit is what separates the good from the great.

Example: Think of a startup founder who continues to push forward to secure funding and grow their business despite numerous setbacks and rejections. They stay focused on their vision, believing in their product even when others don't. Similarly, a student who perseveres through a challenging academic year, or a parent who juggles multiple responsibilities while maintaining a positive outlook, also demonstrate mental toughness in their respective domains.

Adaptability

Adaptability is the ability to adjust to new conditions and pivot when necessary. In a rapidly changing environment, those who can adapt quickly are the ones who thrive.

Example: Consider an athlete who alters their training regimen due to an unexpected injury. Instead of giving up, they find new ways to stay in shape and prepare for their next competition.

Toughness

Toughness is the ability to withstand adversity and remain steadfast in facing challenges. It's about staying strong when others might falter.

Example: Imagine a football team trailing significantly in the Super Bowl. Despite the odds, they stay focused, stick to the game plan, and claw their way back to victory.

Perseverance

Perseverance is the persistence in doing something despite difficulty or delay in achieving success. It's the drive to keep going, even when progress seems slow.

Example: Picture a performer who continues to audition and practice despite initial stage fright and early career failures. Their dedication eventually landed them a leading role on Broadway.

Mental Toughness in Action

1. Staying Focused Under Pressure

Rivals will always try to exploit any perceived weakness, often testing your mental Toughness. Staying focused on your game plan, whether closing a multi-billion dollar deal, winning a Super Bowl game, or stepping on stage for a big performance, is crucial.

Example: An entrepreneur negotiating a pivotal deal must stay calm and collected, not letting the pressure affect their decision-making process. Similarly, a quarterback in a high-stakes game must read the defense and make quick, accurate decisions despite the mounting pressure.

2. The Role of Coaches and Mentors

Coaches and mentors play a pivotal role in nurturing resilience. They offer invaluable guidance, unwavering support, and the occasional tough love that pushes individuals beyond their perceived limits. Their role is not just significant, but indispensable in the journey of developing mental Toughness.

3. Actionable Insight

Actively seek out mentors who challenge you and provide constructive feedback. Their wealth of experience and unique perspective can be instrumental in helping you build mental Toughness. This proactive approach can be a game-changer in your journey towards resilience.

Building a Resilient Mindset

Building resilience is not a one-time task, but an ongoing process that involves cultivating a positive mindset, developing coping strategies, and learning from setbacks. This process empowers you, giving you the tools to navigate life's challenges with confidence and control.

Mental Toughness is a vital attribute that transcends domains, from sports to business to performance arts. By focusing on grit, adaptability, toughness, and perseverance, you can develop the mental Toughness needed to excel in any field. Remember, **the path to success is rarely smooth**, but you can overcome any obstacle with resilience.

Practical Application

In business, professionals can achieve peace of mind by establishing clear goals and maintaining a robust support system enabling them to stay focused amidst uncertainty and make informed decisions without anxiety. In sports, athletes who practice mental Toughness can better manage the pressure of competition, allowing them to perform at their best while enjoying the process. Fostering mental resilience empowers individuals to maintain their composure, cultivate a positive outlook, and experience a harmonious balance in all aspects of their lives. For example, a student can use mental toughness to stay focused during exam preparation, or a performer can use it to manage stage fright and deliver a stellar performance.

Achieving Peace of Mind Through Mental Toughness in Life, Business, and Sports

Mental toughness is a crucial quality that empowers individuals to remain composed and focused amidst challenges in life, business, and sports. This inner strength is developed over time through deliberate practice, resilience, and a strong willpower to overcome adversity.

In life, mental toughness helps individuals manage stress, build robust relationships, and maintain a positive outlook during difficult times.

In the business world, it enables professionals to make critical decisions under pressure, adapt to rapidly changing environments, and persist in the face of competition.

Athletes benefit from mental toughness by enhancing their performance, sustaining their motivation, and recovering quickly from setbacks or failures.

Cultivating this resilience leads to achieving a state of peace of mind where individuals can navigate their personal and professional journeys with clarity and confidence.

Chapter 27

The Joy of the Journey

"Success is not the key to happiness. Happiness is the key to success. If you love what you are doing, you will be successful." — **Albert Schweitzer**

Albert Schweitzer, an esteemed theologian and philosopher, suggests that true success is rooted in passion and contentment. His statement encourages individuals to pursue what they love, as fulfillment leads to greater achievements.

Success is a term that's often thrown around loosely, yet its true essence still needs to be discovered for many. During my life, I came to the conclusion that success gave me "peace of mind."

The "Joy of the Journey" to success emphasizes the value of embracing and appreciating the entire process of achieving goals rather than focusing solely on the result. This perspective encourages individuals to find fulfillment in the daily activities, challenges, and learning opportunities that arise on the path to their objectives. It shifts the emphasis from a distant, often elusive endpoint to the present moments rich with potential for personal growth and enjoyment. By adopting this mindset, people are more likely to savor the small victories and insights gained along the way, including developing new skills, overcoming obstacles, and forming meaningful relationships. This approach makes the journey more enjoyable and helps maintain motivation and resilience as the process becomes a source of satisfaction. Ultimately, understanding and experiencing the joy of the journey can lead to a more balanced, enriched, and sustainable path to success, where the pursuit itself is as rewarding as achieving goals. The "joy of the journey" approach to success significantly differs from a singular focus on the end goal in several key ways:

Process vs. Outcome Orientation

Achieving peace of mind in life, business, and sports can be greatly enhanced by embracing the "joy of the journey." Here are some key points to consider:

1. **Mindfulness and Presence**

- **Focus on the Moment**: Practice mindfulness to appreciate each step of your journey, whether it's daily tasks or training for a competition.

- **Reduce Stress**: Being present can help mitigate anxiety about future outcomes.

2. **Setting Realistic Goals**

- **Process Over Outcome**: Shift your focus from end results to the processes and experiences that lead to those results.

- **Celebrate Small Wins**: Acknowledge and celebrate milestones, no matter how small, to maintain motivation and joy.

3. **Cultivating a Positive Mindset**

- **Embrace Challenges**: View obstacles as opportunities for learning and growth rather than setbacks.

- **Gratitude Practice**: Regularly reflect on what you're grateful for in your journey to foster a positive outlook.

4. **Building Strong Relationships**

- **Support Systems**: Surround yourself with positive influences—friends, mentors, or teammates who encourage you.

- **Community Engagement**: Engage with communities that share your passions, enhancing the journey through shared experiences.

5. Balancing Work and Play

- **Work-Life Harmony**: Strive for balance between professional responsibilities and personal passions to avoid burnout.
- **Find Joy in Hobbies**: Engage in activities that bring you joy outside of work and sports, helping to recharge your mind.

6. Learning and Adaptation

- **Continuous Learning**: Embrace a mindset of lifelong learning; every experience teaches something valuable.
- **Adaptability**: Be open to changing your approach based on experiences, which can lead to greater satisfaction.

7. Reflecting on Progress

- **Journaling**: Keep a journal to reflect on your experiences, thoughts, and feelings as you navigate your journey.
- **Regular Check-Ins**: Periodically assess your goals and feelings to ensure they align with your values and aspirations.

Lessons Learned Along the Way

The road to success is paved with numerous stepping stones and milestones. Here are some important lessons learned on this incredible journey:

1. Every Step Counts

Success is a process. Each small step and each minor achievement contributes to the larger goal. Recognizing and celebrating these incremental wins keeps us motivated and focused.

2. Stay Resilient

The path to success can be challenging. There will be hurdles and setbacks. But remember, resilience is key. Learning from failures and pushing forward despite obstacles builds character and fortitude, making the journey more rewarding.

3. Collaboration is Crucial

Working with others, whether in a business team or a sports squad, teaches the importance of collaboration. Trusting your teammates, leveraging each other's strengths, and working towards a common goal can lead to extraordinary outcomes, fostering a sense of unity and shared success.

4. Adaptability is Essential

Being open to change and adaptable in your approach can make a significant difference. The ability to pivot and make necessary adjustments is often the key to overcoming hurdles and reaching success.

5. Enjoy the Process

It's easy to become fixated on the end goal, but true joy lies in the process. Each moment, effort, and learning experience makes the journey worthwhile. Take time to appreciate the progress and experiences along the way.

The Joy in Every Milestone

Ultimately, the joy of the success journey can be found in every milestone, big or small. It's in the shared laughs, the collective brainstorming sessions, the late-night efforts, and the eventual celebrations. It's in the lessons learned, the resilience, and the relationships formed.

Achieving Peace of Mind in Life, Business, and Sports by Embracing the "Joy of the Journey"

Success—whether in life, business, or sports—isn't just a destination. It's a vibrant, exhilarating experience filled with valuable lessons, memorable moments, and a profound sense of achievement that goes beyond reaching the final goal. This post celebrates the joy found in the journey to success, drawing on personal anecdotes, key lessons learned, and the sheer delight of reaching new heights as part of a team or group.

In life, when you allow yourself to be present in each moment, whether navigating challenges or celebrating victories, you foster a sense of calm that can enhance your overall well-being. This approach encourages mindfulness, reducing stress and anxiety by shifting your focus from what you must accomplish to what you are experiencing right now.

In business, enjoying the process can lead to greater creativity and innovation as you explore ideas without the pressure of immediate results.

Similarly, in sports, appreciating each training session, competition, and team interaction cultivates stronger bonds and drives performance. Ultimately, it's about understanding that the journey itself is a valuable teacher, providing insights and experiences that contribute to a fulfilling life.

Chapter 28

Giving Back

"Service to others is the rent you pay for your room here on earth."
— **Shirley Chisholm**

Politician Shirley Chisholm communicates that giving back through service is an essential duty we owe as global citizens.

Giving back to society through sports is a powerful way to foster community, promote physical and mental health, and instill valuable life lessons. Sports figures and organizations often engage in philanthropic activities, such as hosting charity matches, providing scholarships for young athletes, or setting up sports clinics in underserved areas. These initiatives expand access to sports and help cultivate discipline, teamwork, and leadership among participants. Furthermore, sports can serve as a unifying force, bridging cultural and socioeconomic divides and bringing people together for a common cause. By leveraging the widespread appeal and inclusive nature of sports, athletes and sports organizations can significantly contribute to societal well-being, inspiring participants and spectators to strive for personal and communal growth. Through these efforts, sports become more than just games; they transform into a catalyst for positive social change and community development.

Engaging youth in social initiatives can be both impactful and transformative. Here are some innovative ways to encourage young people to participate in these programs, each of which has the potential to transform lives and inspire hope for a better future:

Digital Integration

- **E-sports and Virtual Competitions**: Leverage gaming's popularity by organizing e-sports tournaments with a cause, such as raising awareness or funds for social issues. Virtual fitness challenges can also engage youth interested in technology.

- **Mobile Apps**: In this digital age, technology plays a crucial role in sports-based social initiatives. Develop apps that track athletic performance and contribute to social causes based on milestones reached, akin to charity miles for runners. This not only encourages physical activity but also fosters a sense of social responsibility among the youth.

Community Leadership Roles

- **Youth Ambassadors**: Empower young athletes by giving them ambassador roles in sports clubs, where they can lead by example and motivate their peers to contribute to community-driven sports events.

- **Peer Coaching**: Implement programs where older youth can train younger children, promoting skills transfer and leadership.

Inclusive Sports Events

- **Unified Sports**: Host events that mix athletes with and without disabilities, promoting inclusivity and empathy among participants.

- **Global Link-Ups**: Use technology to link sports teams worldwide for international tournaments or joint training sessions focused on cultural exchange and global issues.

Educational Workshops

- **Life Skills Through Sports**: Incorporate workshops that teach life skills alongside sports training sessions. These could cover financial literacy, health education, and environmental stewardship, making the sports program more holistic.

- **Career Days**: Integrate sports with career exploration days where professionals from various fields related to sports (such as sports management, coaching, and/or physiotherapy) give talks and workshops.

Cause-Driven Competitions

- **Charity Matches**: Organize sports matches where participation fees or ticket sales go towards a charitable cause. Engage youth in selecting the causes they care about, giving them a sense of ownership and responsibility.

- **Eco-Sports Events**: Create sports events with an environmental focus, such as cleanup runs, where participants collect litter as part of a race, or cycling events promoting sustainable transportation.

Rotary International

- **Scholarships**: Award underprivileged and asset-restricted students scholarships so they can attend college, receive a degree, and thus change their family dynamic forever.

- **Storytelling Sessions**: Invite inspirational speakers from the sports world who have made significant contributions to society to share their stories and can serve as a powerful motivator for young individuals.

Partnerships and Collaborations

- **Corporate Sponsorships**: Partner with local businesses or large corporations to fund sports-based social initiatives. These partnerships can provide resources for better equipment, uniforms, and event hosting, making sports more accessible.

- **Community Service Organizations**: Collaborate with non-profits and service groups that are not directly related to sports but share a common goal of community improvement. This can broaden the impact and reach of both organizations.

Engaging youth in sports-based social initiatives not only promotes physical activity and healthy lifestyles but also instills a profound sense of community responsibility and global citizenship. These innovative approaches ensure that sports serve as a vehicle for positive social change, aligning athletic pursuits with broader societal benefits and fostering a sense of connection and responsibility in the participants. Several sports-based initiatives worldwide have successfully driven positive social change by leveraging sports' universal appeal and community-building power.

Here are a few notable examples:

Right to Play

Overview: Founded by Olympic speed skating champion Johann Olav Koss, Right to Play is an international organization that uses sports and games to educate and empower children facing adversity.

Impact: Operating in multiple countries, the organization reaches over one million children weekly, helping to teach essential life skills, provide educational opportunities, and promote health and well-being through structured play activities.

Magic Bus

Overview: Started in Mumbai, India, Magic Bus uses sports to move children out of poverty by nurturing them on a journey from childhood to livelihood.

Impact: Through activities and curriculum-based sports programs, Magic Bus has impacted over one million children and young people in India, helping them break the cycle of poverty by improving their education, health, and employment prospects.

Peace Players

Overview: This initiative uses basketball to unite and educate young people from divided communities. It was initially founded to bridge racial divides in Northern Ireland and has expanded globally.

Impact: Peace Players has conducted programs in locations including the Middle East, South Africa, Cyprus, and the United States, demonstrating significant improvements in attitudes towards members of other communities among its participants.

Street Soccer USA

Overview: Focused on improving the life skills and personal engagement of homeless and underserved youth through soccer.

Impact: Street Soccer USA organizes leagues in multiple U.S. cities, providing a platform for social inclusion and personal development. Participants have shown improvement in employment status, housing conditions, and mental health.

Surfers, Not Street Children

Overview: This organization combines surfing with mentorship and support to transform the lives of street children in Durban, South Africa, and Mozambique.

Impact: It has been successful in helping children transition from street life to stable situations, with many former street children becoming professional surfers, educators, and advocates within their communities.

Soccer Without Borders

Overview: Soccer Without Borders uses soccer as a vehicle for positive change, providing underserved youth with a toolkit to overcome obstacles to growth, inclusion, and personal success.

Impact: Operating in the USA and abroad, it has effectively engaged refugee and immigrant children, helping them integrate into their new communities through sports and educational support.

Each of these initiatives exemplifies how sports can be more than just a game, acting instead as a powerful tool for social change. By engaging youth in structured sports programs, these organizations address broader social issues such as poverty, social exclusion, and community divisions, proving that sports can effectively contribute to societal improvement and personal development. These success stories serve as inspiration for others to get involved in similar initiatives and make a difference in their communities.

ConNEXTions Foundation

Overview: Providing a blueprint of success for student-athletes, ConNEXTions has been particularly successful in guiding talented male and female student-athletes in all sports to get to the next level in college, professional and Olympic levels

Impact: Founded in Los Angeles, CA, and operating in the USA and abroad, these student athletes' family dynamic has changed in a positive manner for future generations.

ConNEXTions' financial literacy process for these young student-athletes has also significantly impacted their success and happiness in high school and college.

Key Initiatives

At ConNEXTions Foundation, it's crucial to give back to the community when you succeed in business, sports, or through inheritance. This philosophy drives our initiatives to uplift the less fortunate and help them grow and thrive.

Impact Stories

Athletes Giving Back

One of our proudest moments has been watching high school and college athletes who have turned pro come back to their roots and contribute to their communities. These athletes, who have earned significant amounts of money, understand the importance of giving back. They donate financially and invest their time in mentoring younger athletes, guiding them to follow in their footsteps.

Community Builders

Giving back isn't just about money; sometimes, it's about contributing time and resources to create lasting impacts. For instance, a thriving community builder substantially profited from selling recently built homes and donated them to a small park. This park offers a recreational space where new homeowners can enjoy quality time with their children, fostering a sense of community and well-being.

Future Plans

Looking ahead, ConNEXTions Foundation is committed to furthering our community engagement efforts. One of our upcoming initiatives is providing free professional training sessions for student-athletes.

These sessions are designed to help student-athletes secure college scholarships through their athletic abilities and beyond. By investing in these young talents, we are helping them achieve their dreams and building a stronger, more supportive community.

Success Stories from Beneficiaries

From Student-Athlete to Scholar

One inspiring story is that of Lisa Thompson, a former track star at the local high school. With the help of the professional training sessions provided by the ConNEXTions Foundation, Lisa enhanced her athletic skills. She learned essential life skills, such as time management and teamwork. As a result, she secured a full scholarship to a prestigious university, where she continues to excel both academically and athletically, serving as a role model for younger athletes in her community.

Empowering Through Education

Another remarkable beneficiary is Marcus Lee, who participated in our mentorship program. Coming from a challenging background, Marcus received guidance from a professional athlete who helped him understand the importance of education alongside sports. With this support, he improved his grades significantly and earned a scholarship to study sports management. Now, he is determined to give back, aspiring to mentor others who face similar challenges, embodying the spirit of the ConNEXTions Foundation.

Building Dreams

Finally, we celebrate the story of Ana Garcia, who, with the resources provided by our community initiatives, started her own small business after attending our entrepreneurship workshops. Ana's bakery has become a beloved fixture in the neighborhood, providing delicious treats and creating job opportunities for residents. Her journey exemplifies how our efforts can lead to tangible change and inspire others to pursue their entrepreneurial dreams.

Inspiring Leadership

In addition to individual achievements, the ConNEXTions Foundation has fostered a vibrant community of leaders among its participants. Take David Robinson, for instance, who emerged as a natural leader during group activities and workshops. Recognizing his potential, our team encouraged him to take on more responsibilities within the program. David organized various events, facilitating his personal growth and enhancing his peers' experiences. His ability to engage and motivate others has made a significant impact, turning him into a beacon of inspiration for many. Today, David is not only pursuing a degree in community development. Still, he is also actively involved in local initiatives to empower youth in his area, thus embodying the foundation's mission to cultivate leadership and service in every facet of life.

Achieving Peace of Mind by Giving Back to the Community in Life, Business, and Sports

In life, giving back to the community can profoundly enrich one's life and foster a sense of peace and fulfillment. Whether through volunteering, supporting local businesses, or coaching youth sports, these acts of service create meaningful connections and contribute to a more supportive environment.

In business, corporate social responsibility initiatives enhance a company's reputation and foster employee engagement and morale, cultivating a culture of collaboration and empathy.

In sports, athletes who give back by mentoring young players or participating in community events often find that their contributions help them rediscover their passion for the game while inspiring the next generation. This continued cycle of giving and receiving creates a harmonious balance, ultimately leading to a more profound sense of purpose and peace of mind for individuals committed to making a difference.

Chapter 29

Building Your Brand: Modern Day Business-Minded Individuals

"Your brand is what other people say about you when you're not in the room." — Jeff Bezos

The founder of Amazon, Jeff Bezos, emphasizes the importance of perception and reputation in defining your brand's identity and influence. This quote highlights that building a strong brand, much like personal reputation, requires dedication and excellence.

Building your brand in business and sports is not just essential, it's empowering in today's interconnected world. Your first impressions online are not just critical, they're within your control. A strong brand can set you apart in a crowded marketplace, attracting employers, clients, or collaborators who resonate with your unique value proposition. Start by defining your core skills, strengths, and the specific services or expertise you offer. Consistently communicating these through your professional profiles, such as LinkedIn, and your website can establish your reputation as an expert in your field. Create and share relevant content, such as blog posts or case studies, demonstrating your knowledge and contributing to industry discussions. This is your journey, and you're in the driver's seat.

On a personal level, your brand is not just about how you present yourself in everyday interactions and on social media platforms. It's about being authentic and letting your personality shine through. People connect with individuals, not just credentials. Your personal brand is an extension of your values and goals, and aligning your public image with these is key. Engaging genuinely with your community and showing consistency in your personal and professional life reinforces trust and strengthens your relationships. Remember, your personal brand is about you, not just your professional persona.

In both realms, networking plays a crucial role. It's not just about enhancing your visibility and deepening your connections, it's about being part of a community that shares your professional interests and passions. Attend industry conferences, participate in webinars, and join groups that reflect your professional interests and passions. By actively engaging with others, you enhance your visibility and deepen your connections, which can lead to new opportunities and personal growth. Building your brand is an ongoing process of refinement and engagement that, when done well, opens doors and enriches your professional and personal life.

Effectively showcasing your brand on social media involves strategic planning and consistent effort. Here's how you can make the most of various platforms to highlight your brand:

Define Your Brand Identity

- **Know Your Unique Value**: Identify what makes you unique in your chosen field. It could be a specific skill, experience, or perspective.

- **Clarify Your Goals**: Understand what you want to achieve with your social media presence. Are you seeking employment, attracting freelance clients, or establishing yourself as a thought leader?

Professional Networking

- **Visual Storytelling**: Platforms like Instagram and Pinterest are great for creatives who want to showcase their work visually.

- **Dynamic Content**: TikTok and YouTube are excellent for more dynamic, engaging content, especially if your brand benefits from demonstrations or verbal communication.

Create High-Quality Content

- **Align Content With Your Brand**: Whether it's articles, videos, or podcasts, ensure your content consistently reflects your brand's voice and values.

- **Educate and Add Value**: Provide relevant insights, tips, or solutions to your audience and establish your authority and expertise.

Engage Regularly and Authentically

- **Post Consistently**: Use scheduling tools to maintain a regular posting schedule. Consistency keeps your audience engaged and helps build a loyal following.

- **Interact with Followers**: Respond to comments, participate in discussions, and engage with other users' content. Authentic interaction fosters connections and boosts visibility.

Leverage Multimedia

- **Diverse Formats**: Mix text, images, and videos to keep your content fresh and engaging. Each format can appeal to different segments of your audience.

- **Professionalism in Presentation**: Ensure your visuals and overall aesthetics align with your professional image.

Monitor and Adapt

- **Analyze Performance**: Use analytics tools provided by social platforms to track the performance of your posts. Look for patterns in what works and what doesn't.

- **Stay Current**: Keep up-to-date with the latest trends in social media and your industry to keep your content relevant.

Personalize Your Interaction

- **Storytelling**: Share personal stories or experiences that resonate with your professional journey, humanizing your brand and making it more relatable.

- **Customized Content**: Tailor your messages and content according to the demographics and interests of your audience.

Professionalism Across Profiles

- **Consistent Branding**: Using a consistent name, profile picture, and bio across all platforms helps create a recognizable brand identity.

- **Privacy Settings**: Be mindful of your privacy settings and the personal content you share. Keep a healthy boundary between personal and professional posts.

By following these steps, you can effectively showcase your brand on social media, turning your online presence into a powerful personal and professional growth tool.

Tailoring your brand messaging to resonate with a specific target audience is crucial for effective communication and engagement. Here's a structured approach to help you refine your messaging to better connect with your desired audience:

Understand Your Audience

- **Demographic Details**: Gather information on the age, gender, location, education, and income levels of your target audience.

- **Psychographics**: Understanding the values, interests, lifestyle, and challenges of your audience will help you craft messages that speak directly to their needs and aspirations.

- **Behavioral Insights**: Study their buying behaviors, brand loyalties, and product usage patterns to understand what drives their decisions.

Define Your Unique Value Proposition (UVP)

- Clearly articulate what differentiates you from competitors and how it benefits your target audience. Your UVP should address the specific needs or problems of your audience.

Craft Your Message

- **Relevance**: Ensure your message addresses the interests and needs of your target audience. Use language and examples that reflect their everyday experiences.

- **Clarity**: Avoid jargon and complex language. Your message should be easily understandable to ensure it resonates clearly with your audience.

- **Emotion**: Emotional appeal can be a powerful tool. Determine what emotions are relevant to your audience (e.g., security, happiness, success) and weave those into your messaging.

- **Select Platforms Where Your Target Audience is Most Active:** For younger demographics, this might be Instagram or TikTok; whereas LinkedIn might be more appropriate for professional audiences.

- **Tailor the Style and Format of Your Messages** to fit the norms and expectations of each platform while maintaining a consistent brand voice.

Use Engagement Strategies

- **Interactive Content**: Use polls, quizzes, and questions to engage your audience and encourage them to interact with your brand.

- **Storytelling**: People remember stories better than facts. Share stories that illustrate your brand's impact on real people.

- **Call to Action**: Always include a clear call to action that guides your audience to what to do next—whether it's subscribing, contacting you, or purchasing a product.

Gather Feedback and Adapt

- Collect feedback regularly through surveys, comments, and engagement metrics. Listen to what your audience says about your brand.

- Be prepared to tweak your message based on this feedback to ensure it continually resonates with your audience as their preferences and the market evolve.

Maintain Consistency

- Ensure that every piece of content you create and interaction with your audience reinforces your brand message and values. Consistency helps build trust and strengthens your brand identity.

Building a solid personal and professional brand is essential today, where visibility can significantly impact your income. Whether you're an entrepreneur, a career professional, or an athlete, your brand can open doors to new opportunities and elevate your status in your field. Here's a guide to help you build and leverage your brand for success.

Why Building Your Brand Matters

Visibility

A well-crafted brand enhances your visibility, making you more recognizable and trustworthy. It could lead to increased opportunities, whether landing a lucrative business deal, securing a promotion, or attracting sponsorships as an athlete.

Income

Your brand can directly affect your income. A strong brand can lead to more customers and higher sales for entrepreneurs. For career professionals, it can result in job offers and promotions. Thanks to initiatives like NIL (Name, Image, Likeness) agreements, athletes with a solid personal brand can attract endorsements and sponsorships.

Critical Strategies for Building Your Brand

1. Define Your Unique Value Proposition (UVP)

Understand what sets you apart from others in your field. Whether it's a unique skill set, a compelling story, or a distinct approach to your work, your UVP will be the foundation of your brand.

2. Develop a Consistent Online Presence

- **Website**: Create a professional website that showcases your work, achievements, and values.

- **Social Media**: Be active on platforms where your target audience spends their time. Share valuable content, engage with your followers, and maintain a consistent voice.

- **Blogging**: Write articles or create content highlighting your expertise and providing value to your audience.

3. Network Strategically

Build relationships with key influencers and peers in your industry. Attend events, join online forums, and participate in discussions to expand your network.

4. Leverage Media and Public Relations

Get featured in industry publications, podcasts, and interviews. This will not only boost your credibility but also expose you to a broader audience.

5. Personal Branding for Athletes

With the introduction of NIL agreements, athletes can now monetize their brands while still in school. High school and college athletes are paid to use their name, image, and likeness, providing a valuable income stream and increasing visibility.

Success Stories

Many individuals and brands have successfully built their brands in ways that align with these strategies. High school and college athletes are using NIL agreements to their advantage, securing endorsements and sponsorships that were previously unattainable. Entrepreneurs and career professionals who have invested in their brands have seen significant returns in terms of visibility and income.

Athletes like AJ Dybantsa have capitalized on NIL agreements to secure lucrative deals with major brands.

Entrepreneurs like Red Bull have built online solid presences that attract customers and drive sales.

Career Professionals like Lebron James have leveraged their brands to land promotions and industry recognition.

Creating Peace of Mind Through Branding Success in Life, Business, and Sports

Establishing a successful brand opens new avenues and cultivates a profound sense of peace of mind. Having a clear and consistent personal or professional brand fosters confidence in your identity and mission, allowing you to navigate challenges more effectively. Knowing who you are and what you stand for can ease mental burdens and reduce anxiety about external perceptions.

In business, a strong brand can lead to stable relationships and loyalty from clients and partners, mitigating the stress associated with unpredictable market dynamics. For athletes, a well-defined personal brand can translate into meaningful connections and sponsorships, providing financial security and freedom to focus on performance.

Ultimately, the success of your brand contributes significantly to your overall well-being, allowing you to thrive without the constant worry of being overlooked or misunderstood.

Chapter 30

Relationship Building

"As we express our gratitude, we must never forget that the highest appreciation is not to utter words, but to live by them." — **Eleanor Roosevelt**

Eleanor Roosevelt, a former First Lady of the United States and an influential advocate for human rights, emphasizes the importance of living a life that reflects trust.

Build relationships with customers, investors, suppliers, colleagues, employees and your community. Build long term relationships. This is a key to business success, but also a cornerstone of personal growth and emotional well-being. Strong relationships foster trust, collaboration, and mutual respect, which are critical in any successful endeavor. In the workplace, the ability to forge effective connections with colleagues, clients, and stakeholders can lead to enhanced teamwork, smoother communication, and increased opportunities for innovation.

Building strong relationships is essential for achieving peace of mind in various aspects of life. Whether in personal relationships, business environments, or sports, the connections we foster can significantly impact our mental well-being.

In Life: The Foundation of Trust and Support

- **Emotional Support:** Strong personal relationships provide a support system during challenging times. Sharing experiences with friends and family helps alleviate stress and fosters resilience.

- **Communication:** Open and honest communication builds trust, which is crucial for resolving conflicts and misunderstandings.

- **Quality Time:** Spending quality time with loved ones enhances feelings of belonging and security, contributing to overall peace of mind.

In Business: Collaboration and Trust

- **Networking:** Building a network of professional relationships can potentially lead to new opportunities, partnerships, and collaborations that enhance both personal and business growth.

- **Team Dynamics:** A positive work environment, fostered by strong relationships among team members, leads to better collaboration, creativity, and productivity.

- **Conflict Resolution:** Strong relationships facilitate easier conflict resolution, reducing workplace stress and fostering a more harmonious work atmosphere.

In Sports: Team Cohesion and Mental Strength

- **Team Bonding:** In sports, relationships among teammates can enhance performance. A cohesive team is more likely to communicate effectively and support each other during high-pressure situations.

- **Shared Goals:** Working toward common goals fosters a sense of unity and purpose, which can significantly reduce anxiety and improve focus.

- **Mentorship:** Relationships with coaches and mentors provide guidance and encouragement, helping athletes navigate challenges and maintain a positive mindset.

Business Professional Examples

1. Mentorship Opportunities:

- **Scenario**: An individual might start their career under the guidance of a more experienced mentor. Building a strong, trusting relationship with this mentor gives them invaluable advice, guidance, and potentially career-advancing opportunities. The mentor might introduce them to important contacts, recommend them for projects, or endorse their skills, which could accelerate their career development.

2. Collaborative Projects:

- **Scenario**: In a tech startup, a project manager cultivates strong relationships with cross-functional team members, including developers, designers, and marketers. This harmonious relationship facilitates smoother communication and collaboration, leading to successful project outcomes, innovative solutions, and a quicker response to market needs.

3. Client Retention:

- **Scenario**: A sales professional consistently maintains a positive and proactive relationship with clients by regularly checking in, addressing concerns, and offering customized solutions. This approach enhances client satisfaction and increases the likelihood of contract renewals and referrals to other potential clients.

Life Personal Examples

1. Community Support:

- **Scenario**: By actively participating in local community events and building relationships within the neighborhood, an individual gains a network of support. This network can be crucial during personal emergencies or for general assistance, such as sharing resources or looking after each other's homes during absences.

2. **Personal Growth**:

- **Scenario**: Engaging in a hobby group, such as a book club or a hiking group, helps forge friendships based on shared interests. These relationships can enrich an individual's personal life, providing emotional support, enhancing their understanding of different perspectives, and contributing to overall happiness and well-being.

3. **Emotional Resilience**:

- **Scenario**: An individual who maintains solid familial ties and friendships has a reliable support network to turn to during stress or emotional upheaval. This support system can provide emotional comfort and practical help, crucial for overcoming life's challenges.

These examples illustrate that the strength of relationships can significantly impact success and well-being, whether in professional settings or in personal life. Strong, healthy relationships built on trust, mutual respect, and ongoing communication serve as the foundation for collaborative success and personal fulfillment.

Maintaining personal relationships over time requires effort, commitment, and various strategies to keep connections strong and meaningful.

Here are some effective strategies for nurturing and sustaining personal relationships:

Regular Communication

- **Stay in Touch**: Regular check-ins via phone calls, texts, emails, or social media help keep relationships active. Even a simple message saying "thinking of you" can make a big difference.

- **Deep Conversations**: Beyond everyday small talk, engage in deeper conversations that allow both parties to express their thoughts and feelings, building intimacy and understanding.

Quality Time

- **Set Aside Time**: Make it a priority to spend quality time together, whether it's a weekly coffee date, a monthly dinner, or an annual vacation.

- **Shared Activities**: Engage in activities that both parties enjoy, such as hobbies, sports, attending events, or exploring new places together.

Show Appreciation and Support

- **Express Gratitude**: Regularly express appreciation for the other person's presence and contributions to your life. Small gestures of gratitude can reinforce the value of the relationship.

- **Offer Support**: Be there for them during tough times. Offering support during crises or transitions can cement a relationship more deeply.

Resolve Conflicts Constructively

- **Communicate Openly**: When conflicts arise, address them directly and respectfully. Avoid letting resentments build up.

- **Seek Understanding**: Try to understand the other person's perspective before seeking to be understood. This approach facilitates more effective solutions.

Celebrate Achievements Together

- **Acknowledge Important Milestones**: Celebrate each other's achievements, and milestones could range from birthdays and promotions to personal successes like fitness goals or hobbies.

Personal Growth

- **Encourage Development**: Support and encourage each other's personal and professional growth, which may involve discussing aspirations, attending workshops, or providing constructive feedback.

Adapt to Changes

- **Embracing Change**: As people grow, sometimes their needs and circumstances change. Be willing to adapt the relationship to accommodate life transitions such as moving, changing careers, or growing families.

Reciprocity

- **Give and Take**: Ensure that the relationship is balanced where both parties feel they are giving and receiving equally. Reciprocity fosters fairness and satisfaction in relationships.

Shared Values and Goals

- **Align on Core Values**: Having shared values or goals can strengthen bonds. Discussing and aligning on key aspects of life such as family, ethics, and personal ambitions is beneficial.

Digital Tools

- **Utilize Technology**: Use video calls, collaborative apps, or social media to stay connected, especially when physical meetings are challenging due to distance.

Achieving Peace of Mind Through Relationship Building in Life, Business, and Sports

Investing time and effort into building and nurturing relationships across all areas of life is essential for achieving peace of mind. By fostering trust, communication, and collaboration, we can create supportive environments that can and will enhance our well-being and performance, whether in personal life, business, or sports. Prioritizing these connections not only enriches our experiences but also lays the groundwork for a more fulfilling and peaceful life.

Chapter 31

Networking – A Key Task for Building Success

"Networking is about planting relationships, not trying to harvest them." — Dr. Ivan Misner

Networking expert Dr. Ivan Misner advises that building a business involves nurturing long-term relationships rather than seeking immediate benefits.

Networking is not just *a task,* it's a powerful tool that empowers you to **work smarter,** *not* **harder.**

You may have also heard this saying **"If you are** *not* **networking, you are** *not* **working."**

Networking is indeed a crucial element for success across various domains, including life, business, and sports. Here are some key points highlighting its importance:

1. **Opportunities and Connections**

- **Life:** Personal relationships can provide support, mentorship, and opportunities for growth.
- **Business:** Networking opens doors to potential partnerships, collaborations, and potential clients.
- **Sports:** Athletes often rely on connections for coaching, sponsorships, and exposure to scouts.

2. **Knowledge Sharing**

   - **Life:** Engaging with diverse individuals can broaden your perspective and knowledge base.

   - **Business:** Sharing industry insights and best practices can lead to innovation and improved strategies.

   - **Sports:** Learning from experienced athletes and coaches can enhance skills and performance.

3. **Support System**

   - **Life:** A strong network can offer emotional and practical support during challenging times.

   - **Business:** Networking can provide resources and advice when facing obstacles.

   - **Sports:** Teammates and coaches form a crucial support system, fostering motivation and resilience.

4. **Reputation and Credibility**

   - **Life:** Building a positive reputation through networking can lead to further opportunities and trust.

   - **Business:** A solid network can enhance your credibility, making it easier to attract clients and partners.

   - **Sports:** An athlete's reputation can be bolstered by connections with respected figures in the sport.

5. **Collaboration and Teamwork**

   - **Life:** Collaborating with others can lead to creative solutions and personal growth.

   - **Business:** Networking facilitates teamwork and collaboration on projects, enhancing productivity.

- **Sports:** Success in sports often relies on effective teamwork and communication, fostered through networking.

Building your company or brand through networking is a powerful strategy that leverages human connections to foster business growth and enhance brand visibility.

Effective networking involves:

- We are actively participating in industry events.

- I am joining professional groups.

- They engage on platforms like LinkedIn, where meaningful interactions can lead to collaborations, partnerships, and client acquisitions.

By consistently reaching out and connecting with others in your field, you gain valuable insights, stay abreast of industry trends, and increase the likelihood of referrals and recommendations. This communal engagement helps establish credibility and trust, which is essential for any successful brand. Moreover, the relationships built through networking can provide support during challenges and celebrate successes, creating a dynamic community around your brand. In essence, networking isn't just about exchanging business cards; it's about building enduring relationships that enrich your brand's value and expand its reach in tangible, enduring ways.

Building a solid professional network within your industry is crucial for career growth, knowledge exchange, and business development.

Here are effective strategies that can help you cultivate and maintain a robust network:

Attend Industry Conferences and Events

- **Engage Actively:** Try to attend relevant industry conferences, seminars, and networking events to meet peers, leaders, and influencers in your field. Participate in discussions, ask questions, and follow up with contacts after events.

Leverage Social Media Platforms

- **Utilize LinkedIn:** Optimize your LinkedIn profile with a professional photo, detailed work experience, and skills. Post industry-relevant content regularly, join groups, and engage with others' posts.

- **Engage on Twitter and Facebook:** Follow industry leaders and participate in discussions to increase visibility and establish expertise.

Join Professional Associations

- **Get Involved:** Join professional associations and take an active role. Volunteer for committees or speak at events. These roles increase your visibility and credibility within the community.

Offer Value

- **Share Knowledge:** Regularly share insightful articles, research findings, or case studies relevant to your industry. Offering valuable content helps others and establishes you as a thought leader.

- **Help Others:** Whenever possible, always try to provide support, introductions, or advice to peers. Networking is reciprocal; the more you help, the more likely others will return the favor.

Engage in Continuous Learning

- **Stay Updated**: Keep abreast of industry trends, technologies, and skills. Being well-informed makes you a valuable contact within your network.

- **Attend Workshops and Courses**. These can be excellent places to meet like-minded professionals who are looking to expand their skills and network.

Set Networking Goals

- **Be Strategic**: Identify critical individuals within your industry who can be pivotal in your career—set goals for connecting with them through introductions, social media, or industry events.

Follow Up and Keep in Touch

- **Maintain Relationships**: Networking isn't just about making initial contacts; it's also about maintaining those relationships over time. Follow up with new contacts with a thank-you message or an invitation to meet for coffee.

- **Regular Updates**: Keep your network informed about your professional progress and achievements through periodic updates.

Utilize Mentorship

- **Seek Mentors**: Look for mentorship opportunities within your network. Mentors can provide invaluable guidance, introduce you to important contacts, and help you navigate your career path.

- **Be a Mentor**: Offering mentorship can also expand your network, putting you in touch with newcomers in your industry who might have fresh perspectives or connections.

Host or Participate in Webinars and Live Streams

- **Share Expertise**: Hosting or participating in webinars is an excellent way to showcase your knowledge and connect with others interested in your field.

Be Genuine

- **Build Trust**: Authenticity and trustworthiness is critical in building lasting relationships. Be genuine in your interactions, and show a sincere interest in the people you meet.

Maintaining long-term relationships with professional contacts is crucial for success in any career. Here are some practical tips to keep these relationships strong and mutually beneficial:

Regular Communication

- **Stay in Touch**: Regular updates, whether through emails, social media, or phone calls, help keep the relationship active. It can be something other than work-related; sharing articles, industry news, or even wishing them on special occasions can be practical.

- **Newsletters**: Consider sending a periodic newsletter that updates your network on your professional life and insights into your industry.

Provide Value

- **Be Resourceful**: Always look for ways to add value to your contacts through sharing relevant information, offering assistance with a problem, or introducing them to another contact who could help with their needs.

- **Educational Content**: Share knowledge and resources such as webinars, case studies, or research that might interest them.

Meet Regularly

- **Schedule Face-to-Face Meetings**: Whenever possible, arrange face-to-face meetings for coffee, lunch, or events. Personal interactions can strengthen bonds more than virtual communications.

- **Video Calls**: Regular video calls can help maintain a more personal connection than emails or messages for long-distance contacts.

Celebrate Achievements

- **Acknowledge Important Milestones**: Celebrate your contacts' professional milestones such as promotions, project launches, or personal achievements like birthdays and anniversaries. A quick congratulatory message can mean a lot.

Ask for Feedback

- **Seek Advice**: Occasionally, asking for feedback on your projects or decisions can engage your contacts and make them feel valued for their expertise and opinion.

- **Be Open to Suggestions**: Show that you value their input and are willing to learn from their experiences.

Reciprocate

- **Support Their Endeavors**: Attend their events, promote their work on your platforms, or contribute to their projects. Reciprocity is a critical element in sustaining long-term relationships.

- **Be There in Tough Times**: Offer help or just an ear during challenging times. Supporting a relationship during a crisis can significantly strengthen it.

Personal Touch

- **Customize Interactions**: Tailor your communication based on the individual's interests and preferences. Remembering small details from previous conversations can make your interactions more personal and meaningful.

- **Genuine Interest**: Show genuine interest in their career and life. Ask open-ended questions that encourage them to share more about themselves.

Networking Events

- **Invite Them to Eevents**: Extend invitations to networking events or industry meetups. This is a great way to introduce them to others in your network and catch up in a professional setting.

Leverage Technology

- **Use CRM Tools**: Tools like LinkedIn's Relationship section or dedicated CRM software can help you keep track of essential details about your contacts and remind you when to reach out.

Be Consistent

Consistency is Vital: Consistency in connecting and engaging with your network will lead to stronger, more enduring relationships.

Achieving Peace of Mind Through Networking in Life, Business, and Sports

In all areas of life, success is rarely achieved in isolation. Building and maintaining a strong network is essential for leveraging opportunities, gaining support, sharing knowledge, and enhancing one's reputation. Whether in personal endeavors, business ventures, or athletic pursuits, effective networking can significantly impact success.

Networking is crucial in achieving peace of mind, as it expands our circle of support and resources across different domains.

By actively networking, we can build a web of supportive relationships that enhance our confidence and elevate our overall well-being, ensuring we are never alone in our journey.

Chapter 32

Online Networking Platforms

"Connecting with others has the power to transform who we are and what we can achieve." — Michelle Tillis Lederman

Author and networking expert Michelle Tillis Lederman stresses the transformative impact that meaningful connections have on personal and business growth.

Leveraging online networking platforms will significantly enhance your brand awareness and establish you as a thought leader in your industry.

Online networking platforms can significantly enhance success in life, business, and sports by facilitating connections, collaboration, and opportunities. Here are some key platforms tailored to each area:

For Business

1. LinkedIn

- Ideal for professional networking, job searching, and sharing industry insights.
- Features: Member profiles, connections, endorsements, and professional groups.

2. Meetup

- Helps find and join groups of people with similar interests or professional goals.
- Great for networking events and local meetups.

3. Xing

- Popular in Europe, especially in German-speaking countries.
- Focuses on professional networking and job opportunities.

For Sports

1. Strava

- A social network for athletes, particularly runners and cyclists.
- Users can share workouts, join challenges, and connect with other athletes.

2. TeamSnap

- Designed for sports teams to manage schedules, communicate, and coordinate events.
- Useful for coaches, players, and parents.

3. Sports Engine

- A platform for youth sports organizations to manage teams, registrations, and communication.
- Helps connect families with local sports opportunities.

For Life and Personal Development

1. Facebook Groups

- A versatile platform for joining communities focused on personal growth, hobbies, or professional development.
- Engaging discussions and resources are often shared.

2. Reddit

- Various sub-reddits cater to personal development, business advice, and sports discussions.

- A wealth of information from diverse perspectives.

3. Discord

- Originally for gamers, now used for various communities including business and sports.
- Offers voice, video, and text chat for real-time interaction.

General Networking

1. Twitter (X)

- Great for real-time discussions and connecting with industry leaders.
- Use hashtags to find and engage with relevant communities.

2. Slack

- While primarily a workplace tool, many communities use Slack for networking and collaboration.
- Ideal for niche groups and industry-specific discussions.

3. Clubhouse

- An audio-based social media network where users can join discussions on various topics.
- Offers opportunities to connect with thought leaders in real-time.

Tips for Success

- **Engage Actively:** Participate in discussions, share insights, and ask questions.
- **Build Relationships:** Focus on building genuine connections rather than just collecting contacts.

- **Leverage Content:** Share valuable content relevant to your field to establish yourself as a thought leader.

- **Follow Up:** Maintain connections through follow-up messages or meetings.

By carefully selecting influencers who align with your brand's values and goals and fostering genuine partnerships, you can significantly amplify your brand's reach and impact in your industry.

In the sports industry, influencer collaborations have proven highly effective, leveraging athlete endorsements and partnerships with sports influencers on digital platforms. Here are a few examples of successful influencer collaborations that you could model:

Nike and Cristiano Ronaldo

- **Overview**: Cristiano Ronaldo, one of the most famous football players globally, has a long-standing partnership with Nike. This collaboration includes unique edition products, personalized football boots, and extensive social media sharing.

- **Impact**: Ronaldo's massive following and influence has helped Nike solidify its brand among football enthusiasts and general sports fans worldwide, enhancing sales and brand loyalty.

Under Armour and Stephen Curry

- **Overview**: Under Armour signed Stephen Curry in 2013 and he has since become the face of their basketball line. The collaboration includes the exclusive Curry brand of shoes and apparel.

- **Impact**: This partnership boosted Under Armour's sales and significantly improved its brand visibility and status in the basketball community.

Adidas and Lionel Messi

- **Overview**: Adidas has collaborated with Lionel Messi for many years, creating a line of Messi-branded football boots and featuring him prominently in its marketing campaigns.

- **Impact**: Messi's global appeal and status as one of the greatest football players have greatly enhanced Adidas's market share in football gear.

Red Bull and Extreme Sports Athletes

- **Overview**: Red Bull has effectively used influencer marketing by sponsoring extreme sports athletes in various disciplines, such as snowboarding, BMX, and motorsports.

- **Impact**: These partnerships help cement Red Bull's image as a high-energy, adventurous brand closely aligned with the extreme sports lifestyle.

Gatorade and Serena Williams

- **Overview**: Gatorade has featured Serena Williams in many campaigns, emphasizing perseverance, strength, and hydration in sports.

- **Impact**: Serena's influence extends beyond tennis, touching on empowerment and peak performance themes, which aligns well with Gatorade's branding.

Fitbit and Dean Karnazes

- **Overview**: Ultramarathon runner Dean Karnazes partnered with Fitbit to promote the brand's fitness trackers, participating in challenges and sharing his training data.

- **Impact**: This collaboration showcases the practical use of Fitbit in training regimes, making the product a must-have for serious runners and fitness enthusiasts.

Tips for Modeling Your Influencer Collaborations

- **Align Values and Audience**: Choose influencers whose values and audience align closely with your brand, ensuring authenticity in the partnership, which is crucial for sports fans.

- **Create Exclusive Content**: Develop unique content, such as special editions or behind-the-scenes training footage that can only be accessed through your collaboration.

- **Leverage Multi-Platform Engagement**: Utilize various platforms (Instagram, YouTube, Twitter) to maximize reach and engagement, tailoring content to each platform's strengths.

- **Focus on Storytelling**: Stories of triumph, struggle, and perseverance will impact sports. Use storytelling in your campaigns to create a deeper emotional connection with the audience.

Achieving Peace of Mind Through Online Networking Platforms in Life, Business, and Sports

In today's digital age, online networking platforms have emerged as vital tools for fostering connections across personal, business, and athletic domains. These platforms provide a unique opportunity to engage with diverse communities without the geographical limitations of traditional networking.

For individuals seeking personal growth, platforms like social media groups or online forums allow for shared learning experiences and emotional support, reducing feelings of loneliness.

In the business landscape, professional sites such as LinkedIn empower users to build extensive networks, showcase their expertise, and connect with potential mentors and collaborators. These connections can lead to significant career advancements, allowing professionals to navigate their paths confidently.

For athletes, online platforms facilitate interactions with fellow competitors, coaches, and sponsors, helping cultivate relationships beyond local competitions. By utilizing these digital networking resources, individuals across various fields can strengthen their support systems, mitigate stressors, and pursue their ambitions with renewed peace of mind.

By utilizing these platforms effectively, you can expand your network, gain insights, and unlock new opportunities in business, sports, and personal growth.

Chapter 33

Gratitude

"Gratitude is the inheritance of a noble soul." — Caroline Norton

Caroline Norton, a prominent 19th-century English social reformer and writer, conveys the idea that gratitude is a lasting heritage for those with grace and dignity, highlighting its timeless value in character and society.

Gratitude is not just a feeling of appreciation, it's a transformative power that can enhance mental well-being and foster a sense of interconnectedness with others and the world. It's a cornerstone of positive psychology, often credited to external sources. Practicing gratitude involves recognizing the blessings we often take for granted, from a supportive family and good health to more minor daily comforts like a warm meal or a kind gesture from a stranger.

Gratitude is a powerful tool that can enhance our experiences and lead to greater success across various areas of life. Here's how it plays a role in life, business, and sports.

1. Gratitude in Life

Benefits:

- **Mental Well-Being**: Practicing gratitude can improve mood and reduce stress. Keeping a gratitude journal helps individuals focus on positive aspects of their lives.

- **Stronger Relationships**: Expressing gratitude strengthens bonds with family and friends, fostering a supportive network.

- **Increased Resilience**: A grateful mindset encourages resilience during challenging times, promoting a positive outlook.

How to Practice:

- **Daily Reflection**: Spend a few minutes each day reflecting on what you're thankful for.
- **Express Thanks**: Verbally acknowledge the contributions of others in your life.

2. Gratitude in Business

Benefits:

- **Enhanced Workplace Culture**: A culture of gratitude can lead to higher employee morale and job satisfaction.
- **Improved Team Collaboration**: When team members feel appreciated, they are more likely to collaborate effectively and contribute positively.
- **Creating Better Customer Relationships**: Expressing gratitude to customers can increase loyalty and encourage repeat business.

How to Practice:

- **Recognition Programs**: Implement programs that recognize employees' efforts and achievements.
- **Thank You Notes**: Encourage team members to send thank-you notes to clients or colleagues.

3. Gratitude in Sports

Benefits:

- **Team Cohesion**: Athletes who express gratitude towards teammates and coaches foster a sense of unity and trust.

- **Enhanced Performance**: Grateful athletes often exhibit higher levels of motivation and focus, which in turn leads to improved performance.
- **Positive Mindset**: Gratitude helps athletes manage pressure and stay grounded during competitions.

How to Practice:

- **Post-Game Reflection**: After games, reflect on what went well and thank teammates for their contributions.
- **Mentorship**: Acknowledge the influence of coaches and mentors, fostering a culture of respect and appreciation.

Incorporating gratitude into your daily routine is simpler than you might think and can significantly enhance your overall well-being.

Here are several practical ways to weave gratitude into the fabric of your everyday life:

Keep a Gratitude Journal

- **Daily Entries**: Start or end your day by writing down three things you are grateful for. These can be as significant as family support or as simple as enjoying a sunny day.

Gratitude Reminders

- **Set Reminders**: Use your smartphone or sticky notes to set reminders to pause and reflect on something you are grateful for at specific times during the day.

Mindful Meals

- **Mealtime Reflections**: Before eating, express gratitude for the food, considering the effort of those who grew, transported, and prepared it.

Gratitude Jar

- **Collect Moments**: Keep a jar where you can drop notes of gratitude. This is a fun and visual way of collecting happy moments and appreciation, which you can review at the end of the year or whenever you need a boost.

Gratitude Visits or Letters

- **Express Thanks**: Write a letter to someone who has made a positive difference in your life but whom you've never properly thanked. You can choose to send it or read it out loud to them.

Mindful Meditation

- **Focus on Gratitude**: Incorporate gratitude into your meditation practice by focusing on things you are thankful for, from your body and health to your relationships and experiences.

Digital Gratitude

- **Social Media Posts**: Use your social media platforms to share what you're grateful for or send thanks to friends, family, or colleagues.

Gratitude in Communication

- **Start with Thanks**: In emails and meetings, thank participants for their time or contributions. This sets a positive tone for the interaction.

Random Acts of Kindness

- **Pay it Forward**: Engage in random acts of kindness and be mindful of the joy or relief they bring to others. This will increase your own feelings of gratitude.

Reflective Walks

- **Nature Walks**: Take regular walks in nature, intentionally observing and appreciating the beauty around you. Reflect on the peace or joy these surroundings bring.

Gratitude in Challenges

- **Find the Silver Lining**: When faced with challenges, reflecting on what the situation might be teaching you or how it might be helping you grow is a powerful tool. This practice of gratitude can help you navigate difficult times with a more positive outlook, promoting resilience and personal growth.

Achieving Peace of Mind Through Gratitude in Life, Business, and Sports

Incorporating gratitude into daily practices can lead to profound improvements in personal well-being, professional success, and athletic performance. By taking the time to recognize and appreciate the contributions of others, we not only enhance our own lives but also create a positive ripple effect in our communities, workplaces, and sports teams.

In daily life, cultivating gratitude encourages us to focus on the positives, enhancing our overall emotional resilience and enabling us to navigate challenges with a more optimistic outlook.

In the business world, expressing gratitude towards colleagues, mentors, and clients strengthens professional relationships. It fosters a collaborative environment, leading to increased job satisfaction and productivity.

For athletes, recognizing and appreciating the support from coaches, teammates, and fans can enhance motivation and bolster confidence, ultimately improving performance. By integrating gratitude into our routines, we create a mindset that promotes well-being and fulfillment, affirming our value and the meaningful connections we share with others.

Chapter 34

Giving Oneself Selfless Success

"We make a living by what we get, but we make a life by what we give." — **Winston Churchill**

Winston Churchill articulates the idea that personal success is defined not by wealth or possessions but by the contributions one makes to the lives of others.

The Art of Giving Oneself in Life, Business, and Sports

In a world often driven by individual accomplishments and personal gain, "selfless success" stands out as a beacon of sustainable achievement and fulfillment. This approach emphasizes giving oneself for the greater good, whether in life, business, or sports. Here, we explore the key themes of servant leadership, generosity, and teamwork, which form the foundation of selfless Success.

Servant Leadership

What is Servant Leadership?

Servant leadership is a philosophy where the leader's primary goal is to serve others. This contrasts with traditional leadership, where the main focus is the thriving of the company or organization. Leaders who practice servant leadership prioritize their team's well-being and development, fostering a supportive and empowering environment.

Why it Matters

- **Enhanced Team Performance**: When leaders prioritize their team's needs, it creates a motivated and committed workforce.

- **Trust Building**: Servant leaders build trust by showing genuine concern for their team members' well-being.

- **Sustainable Success**: Organizations led by servant leaders tend to have lower employee turnover and higher long-term Success.

Real-World Examples

- **Business**: Howard Schultz, former CEO of Starbucks, is known for his servant leadership style, which emphasizes employee welfare and an inclusive company culture.

- **Sports**: Phil Jackson, the legendary NBA coach, practiced servant leadership by prioritizing his players' personal and professional growth, leading to multiple championships.

The Power of Generosity

Generosity, in this context, goes beyond financial giving. It encompasses sharing time, knowledge, and resources to support others' growth and Success. Generosity fosters a culture of abundance and gratitude, which can transform personal relationships, business environments, and team dynamics.

Benefits of Generosity

- **Enhanced Relationships**: Generous actions build stronger, more meaningful connections between individuals.

- **Positive Organizational Culture**: In business, a culture of generosity leads to higher employee satisfaction and loyalty.

- **Increased Team Morale**: In sports, generous teammates who share their skills and support others create a cohesive and high-performing team.

Ways to Practice Generosity

- **In Life**: Volunteer for community services, mentor someone, or offer a listening ear to those in need.

- **In Business**: Share business insights with peers, provide mentorship programs and recognize employees' efforts.

- **In Sports**: Support teammates' development, share training techniques, and celebrate others' successes as your own.

The Essence of Teamwork

Teamwork is about working collaboratively with others to achieve a common goal. It involves mutual respect, shared responsibilities, and effective communication. Successful teams leverage each member's unique strengths, creating a synergy that leads to more extraordinary accomplishments than any one individual may achieve alone.

Importance of Teamwork

- **Innovation and Creativity**: Diverse teams bring multiple perspectives, leading to innovative solutions and creative problem-solving.

- **Shared Burden**: Team members support each other, distributing workloads and reducing stress.

- **Achieving Goals**: Effective teamwork aligns everyone's efforts towards a common objective, ensuring that goals are achieved efficiently.

Building Strong Teams

- **Foster Open Communication with Others**: Encourage honest and transparent communication with others to build trust and understanding among team members.

- **Define Clear Roles for Everyone**: Ensure everyone knows their responsibilities and how they contribute to the team's Success.

- **Celebrate Success Together vs. Individually**: Recognize and celebrate individual and team achievements to reinforce a sense of unity and shared purpose.

Life

Giving of oneself in one's personal life can lead to significant improvements in mental well-being. Volunteering for community service or helping a friend can create a deep sense of fulfillment and purpose. Giving fosters connections nurtures relationships, and cultivates empathy, which are essential components for achieving peace of mind.

Business

In the business realm, offering support and guidance to colleagues enhances team dynamics. It instills a sense of belonging and security within the workplace. By prioritizing collaborative efforts and recognizing the contributions of others, individuals can cultivate a positive atmosphere that promotes well-being. This yields greater job satisfaction and contributes to overall mental peace.

Sports

Teamwork and giving back to teammates are crucial in fostering a harmonious environment in sports. Encouraging others, sharing knowledge, and celebrating victories collectively can create bonds beyond the game. This camaraderie improves performance and brings a profound sense of contentment and peace of mind as athletes feel valued and part of something greater than themselves.

Creating success by giving oneself fully in life, business, and sports involves a blend of dedication, passion, and a willingness to serve others. Here are some key principles to consider:

1. **Commitment to Goals**

    - Set clear, achievable goals.
    - Remain committed to these set goals, even when faced with challenges.

2. **Embrace a Growth Mindset**

    - View failures as opportunities for learning.
    - Continuously seek to improve your skills and knowledge.

3. **Serve Others**

    - In business, prioritize customer satisfaction and employee well-being.
    - In sports, always support teammates and foster a positive environment.

4. **Discipline and Hard Work**

    - Consistently put in the effort required to excel.

- Develop routines that will enhance your productivity and performance.

5. **Balance and Well-Being**

    - Maintain a healthy work-life balance to prevent burnout.
    - Invest time in self-care, mental health, and personal relationships.

6. **Networking and Relationships**

    - Build strong relationships within your industry or sport.
    - Collaborate and share knowledge with others to foster a supportive community.

7. **Resilience**

    - Cultivate resilience to bounce back from setbacks.
    - Stay focused on your long-term vision, even when immediate results are not visible.

8. **Adaptability**

    - Be open to change and willing to pivot when necessary.
    - Stay informed about trends and shifts in your field or sport.

Look at What is Built and Accomplished by Giving

Building Trust

- **Reliability and Support**: When individuals consistently give of themselves, whether through volunteering, helping neighbors, or participating in community projects, they establish reliability and trustworthiness. Trust is the foundation of any strong community, making it easier for people to rely on one another during good and challenging times.

Encouraging Reciprocity

- **Cultivating a Culture of Giving**: Self-giving sets a precedent and often encourages others to act similarly. This reciprocity multiplies the initial act's impact and weaves a tighter network of support and assistance within the community.

Reducing Social Barriers

- **Inclusivity and Understanding**: Giving oneself often involves crossing social, economic, and cultural barriers to help others. Such cultural interactions can break down prejudices and misconceptions, fostering a more inclusive community where diversity is celebrated and respected.

Enhancing Social Capital

- **Networks and Connections**: Through giving, individuals expand their social networks. These networks become valuable resources that members can draw upon, leading to increased social capital, essential for community development and resilience.

Promoting Collective Well-Being

- **Health and Happiness**: Research shows that giving and altruism are linked to better physical and mental health, not just for the recipient but also for the giver. A healthier community is invariably happier, and happier communities are more cohesive.

Modeling Positive Behavior

- **Influence and Inspiration**: Individuals who give of themselves often inspire and influence others, especially younger generations, to adopt similar behaviors. This modeling of positive behavior helps perpetuate a cycle of generosity and kindness within the community.

Strengthening Community Identity and Pride

- **Shared Goals and Successes**: Collective efforts in community projects or relief efforts contribute to a stronger community identity and pride. Successes achieved together are celebrated as communal victories, reinforcing a collective identity and enhancing social bonds.

Facilitating Conflict Resolution

- **Empathy and Cooperation**: The compassion and understanding required to give oneself aid in resolving conflicts or misunderstandings within the community. Communities can foster a more cooperative environment by focusing on common goals and mutual benefits.

Economic Benefits

- **Support and Sustainability**: Acts of giving can also have economic implications, such as supporting local businesses or aiding those in financial distress, contributing to the overall economic stability and sustainability of the community.

Creating a Legacy of Compassion

- Long–term Impact: A community's culture of giving can leave a lasting legacy, shaping its character and guiding its future interactions and developments.

Creating Success and Peace of Mind by Giving Oneself in Life, Business, and Sports

Success is often a collective journey. By giving yourself fully and prioritizing the well-being of others, you create a foundation for sustainable success in life, business, and sports. Embrace the process and celebrate both individual and collective achievements.

By weaving these threads of self-giving into the fabric of community life, individuals contribute to a more robust, more cohesive social structure that can withstand the challenges it faces while prospering together.

Chapter 35

Two Critical Life Decisions: Profession and Partner

My good friend and teammate, **Jeff Loughery**, has always impacted young people's lives. Jeff would especially state to my three daughters and his students the importance and thought needed when making these two critical decisions. Choosing a profession and selecting a life partner are two of the most pivotal decisions in a person's life, each carrying profound implications for one's future.

Opting for a profession through college or entrepreneurship is a decision that not only shapes professional opportunities and influences personal growth but also has a long-term impact on one's socioeconomic status. The choice demands careful consideration of one's passions, career prospects, and the financial implications of higher education. Similarly, choosing a life partner is a deeply personal decision that profoundly affects emotional well-being and has long-lasting effects on one's personal life and social dynamics.

On the other hand, choosing a life partner is a deeply personal decision that profoundly affects emotional well-being and has long-lasting effects on one's personal life and social dynamics. This choice, more than any other, necessitates a deep understanding of oneself and the ability to plan for the future. It requires introspection and compatibility assessment on countless levels, including values, goals, and mutual respect and understanding. Though vastly different, both decisions demand a high level of self-awareness and foresight, as they significantly sculpt the landscape of one's life journey, impacting nearly every facet of future happiness and stability.

Choosing a profession and selecting a life partner are monumental decisions that significantly impact one's life trajectory. Both require deep reflection and careful consideration of various factors:

Profession

1. Interest and Passion

- **Personal Interest**: Choose a field that genuinely interests you, as this is what you'll be spending a significant amount of time studying and possibly working in.

2. Career Prospects

- **Job Market**: Consider the demand for professionals in your chosen field and the post-graduation career opportunities.

- **Income Potential**: Research potential earnings in your field to ensure it meets your financial goals and lifestyle expectations.

3. Academic Strengths

- **Skill Alignment**: Align your professional choice with your academic strengths and learning style to increase your chances of success and satisfaction.

4. Choosing Between College and Entrepreneurship

- **Affordability**: Evaluate the cost of the degree and weigh it against the potential financial return, considering student loans and possible debt.

- **College Can Provide Valuable Soft Skills and Connections** that can help your business. It can be challenging to enter some fields with a degree.

5. **Institution Reputation**

- **Accreditation and Quality**: Choose a reputable institution recognized for excellence in your chosen field to enhance your qualifications.

Entrepreneurship Field

- When it comes to choosing a profession, it's crucial to select one that ignites your passion and aligns with your core values. This alignment is not just important, it's crucial for finding fulfillment in your professional life. Determine if there is a need for your product and service, and if there is, you're on the right track. Skipping college can give you a head start on your business.

- Communication, problem-solving, and time management are the top skills required for starting a business.

Choosing Professional Career

Before thinking about leaving your job or skipping college, think about what problem you will be solving. Rolling right into entrepreneurship, disregarding education, works for some people but only for some.
This comprehensive approach will help you understand the details of each profession and how they align with your personal and professional aspirations, leading to a more informed and satisfactory career choice.

The turning point for choosing a career starts during the pre-university or university era. In this period, when individuals experience difficulties in their psychological and social lives, asking them to make decisions that will affect their entire lives will increase their stress and prevent them from making sound decisions. During the high school years, individuals who do not yet fully know themselves and cannot identify their advantages, shortcomings, opportunities, and the dangers their choices will cause may have to choose a profession and career unsuitable for them later.

Life Partner

The Most Important Areas When Choosing a Life Partner Are:

- Philosophy on how to raise children and if you both desire to be parents.

- Religious beliefs.

- Financial goals and principles – one of you is very conservative on spending, and the other spends over their means.

1. Values and Beliefs

- **Core Values**: Ensure that your core values and those of your potential partner are aligned. Differences in fundamental beliefs can lead to conflicts.

2. Communication

- **Openness and Honesty**: A strong relationship will be built on the ability to communicate openly and resolve conflicts constructively.

3. Life Goals

- **Future Aspirations**: Partners should have compatible or complementary career, family, and lifestyle goals

4. Emotional Maturity

- **Responsibility and Growth**: Both partners should demonstrate emotional maturity, which includes the ability to manage emotions, take responsibility, and commit to personal growth.

5. Mutual Respect and Support

- **Encouragement and Support**: Look for a partner who respects and supports your personal and professional ambitions.

6. Physical and Emotional Connection

- **Compatibility**: A strong physical and emotional connection involves attraction, affection, and deep connection.

7. Trust and Loyalty

- **Reliability**: Trust is the most important foundation in any relationship, characterized by honesty, faithfulness, and reliability.

Determining whether a potential life partner's values and beliefs are compatible with your own is crucial for long-term relationship success.

Achieving Peace of Mind with Your Professional Career and Life Partner

Choosing the right profession and life partner is crucial for achieving peace of mind, as both decisions significantly influence one's overall happiness and success. They select a profession that aligns with their values, interests, and strengths, fostering fulfillment and enhancing motivation and resilience in overcoming challenges.

Similarly, a supportive life partner is vital in grounding an individual, offering emotional stability, and encouraging personal growth. In business and sports, the synergy between team members or partners can elevate performance while promoting a culture of trust and collaboration.

By thoughtfully considering these choices and ensuring they align with personal values, interests, and strengths, individuals can create a harmonious environment that nurtures personal and professional aspirations, ultimately leading to a more peaceful and satisfying life.

Chapter 36

Entrepreneurship

"Your time is limited, so don't waste it living someone else's life."
— Steve Jobs

Steve Jobs, co-founder of Apple Inc., stresses the importance of authenticity and following one's own vision in the entrepreneurial journey, inspiring leaders to value their individuality and unique contributions to the world.

The Unmatched Value of "TIME" through Entrepreneurial Freedom

The Essence of Entrepreneurial Freedom

When it comes to entrepreneurship, it's not just about financial success, innovation, and leadership. One of the most undervalued yet immensely fulfilling aspects is *the freedom to design your schedule*. This unique benefit can transform your business and your quality of life in ways that other professions simply can't match.

The Priceless Nature of Time

Time is the one resource we all have in equal measure, yet how we use it can vary dramatically. For entrepreneurs, the ability to decide how to allocate time is invaluable. Unlike traditional 9-to-5 jobs, where external schedules and expectations primarily dictate your day, entrepreneurship offers the unique freedom to mold your day to fit your needs, priorities, and aspirations.

Flexibility Equals Productivity

Having a flexible schedule could lead to procrastination or inefficiency. However, for most entrepreneurs, the opposite is true. The flexibility to work during peak productivity hours, take breaks when needed, and create an environment that suits your style can significantly enhance productivity and job satisfaction.

Work-Life Balance

Another crucial benefit of setting your schedule is achieving a better work-life balance by working fewer hours; it means having the flexibility to decide when and where you work. For example, you can attend your child's school event without worrying about missing work or take a mid-day break for a workout to refresh your mind and body. This flexibility reduces stress and improves overall well-being. As a parent and husband, organizing the weekly schedule each Sunday:

- You should have a daily workout schedule. Good health would benefit your wife, kids, or business.

- Schedule a weekly date with your partner. Continuing dating during a relationship is essential to experiencing quality time together.

- Schedule your kids' key activities—birthdays, games. Don't miss these critical activities; they create a lifetime of memories. Remember, the two things children need are your love and your time—everything else will fall into place if you give them these two things.

- Schedule your work appointments—yes, after #1, #2, and #3, you will be shocked to realize that after a while, everything works out.

The Power of Choice

At its core, entrepreneurial freedom is about choice. The choice to start your day at 5 AM or 10 AM, work from a bustling café or the comfort of your home, spend four hours on strategic planning, or two hours on customer meetings. This power to choose is truly liberating.

Real-Life Examples

Sarah's Story

Sarah, the founder of a digital marketing agency, starts her day with a yoga session at 8 AM, followed by a couple of hours of deep work on client strategies. Post-lunch, she dedicates time to team meetings and business development activities. By 5 PM, she's free to pick up her kids and spend quality family time, resuming work for an hour after dinner if needed.

The Intangible Benefits

While financial success is the metric of entrepreneurship, the intangible benefits of setting your own schedule cannot be overstated. These include:

- **Increased Satisfaction**: Knowing you control your day fosters a sense of satisfaction and accomplishment.

- **Reduced Stress**: Flexibility allows you to manage stress better, as you can adjust your schedule to meet personal and professional demands.

- **Enhanced Creativity**: Freedom to work in environments that inspire you can lead to more innovative ideas and solutions.

Call Your Schedule and Take Control

One of the most critical aspects of success is the ability to manage your own time effectively. Whether you're an entrepreneur, an athlete, or simply striving for personal growth, taking control of your schedule allows you to focus on what truly matters.

- Entrepreneurship: Manage your daily tasks, meetings, and deadlines to ensure you always progress toward your business goals.

- Life: Prioritize personal responsibilities, relationships, and self-care to maintain a balanced and fulfilling life.

- Sports: Create a training regimen that enhances your skills and builds your endurance, ensuring you're always at the top of your game.

Tips for Effective Schedule Management

- Use digital tools like calendars and productivity apps.

- Set clear, achievable goals for each day, week, and month.

- Allocate time for rest and recovery to avoid burnout.

You Are Responsible for Success and Failure

Own Your Outcomes

Taking responsibility for your successes and failures is not just a part of growth and improvement; it's a cornerstone of entrepreneurship. This principle encourages a mindset of accountability and self-reflection, making you the master of your own destiny.

- Entrepreneurship: Understand that your business's success relies on your decisions and actions. Learn from failures to make better choices in the future.

- Life: Accept that your happiness and fulfillment are in your hands. Make conscious decisions that align with your values and aspirations.

- Sports: Recognize that your performance results from your effort, discipline, and strategy. Use failures as learning opportunities to refine your approach.

Tips for Building Accountability

- Reflect on your daily actions and their outcomes.

- Seek feedback from mentors, peers, and coaches.

- Create a support system that holds you accountable for your goals.

Inspire and Guide

Leadership is about inspiring and guiding others toward a common goal. Effective leadership is crucial for success, whether leading a team, a company, or even yourself.

- Entrepreneurship: Lead your team with vision and purpose. Foster a culture of innovation and collaboration.

- Life: Be a role model for your family and community. Lead by example and encourage others to reach their potential.

- Sports: Motivate your teammates and push them to achieve collective success. Demonstrate resilience, sportsmanship, and dedication.

Create Innovative Ideas and Products

Innovate and Create

Innovation is the engine of progress. Creating unique ideas and products can set you apart and drive your success forward.

- Entrepreneurship: Continuously seek ways to improve your products or services. Stay ahead of market trends and customer needs.

- Life: Find creative solutions to personal challenges. Enhance your lifestyle with innovative habits and mindsets.

- Sports: Innovate your training techniques and strategies. Stay adaptable and open to new approaches that can enhance your performance.

Tips for Fostering Innovation

- Encourage a culture of creativity and experimentation.

- Stay curious and continuously seek new knowledge.

- Collaborate with diverse individuals to gain different perspectives.

Achieving Peace of Mind and Optimal Success Through Entrepreneurship in Life, Business, and Sports

Success in entrepreneurship is a journey that requires a blend of passion, strategy, and perseverance.

Success in various facets of life—entrepreneurship, personal growth, and sports—can lead to a profound sense of peace of mind. In entrepreneurship, building a successful business fulfills professional aspirations.

Peace of mind contributes to financial stability and personal satisfaction and, in turn, fosters a balanced lifestyle where stress will be effectively managed. Setting and achieving personal goals cultivates self-esteem and confidence, allowing for greater overall happiness.

Similarly, in sports, the discipline of training and the thrill of competition build resilience and teamwork, enhancing mental and physical well-being. By harmonizing achievements across these areas, individuals can create a fulfilling existence that promotes tranquility and contentment.

Chapter 37

Resiliency

"Do not judge me by my success, judge me by how many times I fell down and got back up again." — Nelson Mandela

Resilience and Progress: The Power of Not Giving Up

In today's fast-paced world, resilience is your greatest asset. It's the key to overcoming obstacles, solving problems quickly, and continuously moving forward. Resilience isn't just about bouncing back from failures—it's about leveraging those mistakes to fuel your progress.

The Importance of Resilience

Resilience is the ability to adapt to adversity and keep pushing forward, no matter your challenges. It's not just about recovering from setbacks; it's about emerging stronger and more empowered. In business and sports, as in life, resilience is essential for long-term success. Without it, even the most minor hurdles can feel insurmountable.

Why is Resilience Crucial?

- **Problem-Solving:** Resilient individuals tackle problems head-on and find solutions quickly, minimizing disruption.

- **Adaptability:** They easily adjust to new circumstances and challenges, maintaining momentum.

- **Confidence:** Overcoming obstacles builds self-assurance, making future challenges less daunting.

- **Growth:** Each setback provides valuable lessons contributing to personal and professional development.

Solving Problems Quickly

When faced with a problem, the quicker you can identify and implement a solution, the less impact it will have on your progress. This proactive approach ensures you stay on track, avoiding unnecessary delays or setbacks.

Steps to Solve Problems Efficiently:

1. **Identify the Issue:** Clearly define the problem. What is the root cause?

2. **Generate Solutions:** Brainstorm potential fixes. Be bold and think outside the box.

3. **Evaluate Options:** Assess the pros and cons of each solution. Which is the most feasible and practical?

4. **Implement the Solution:** Take action. Execute the plan with confidence.

5. **Monitor and Adjust:** Check the results. If the problem persists, be prepared to tweak your approach.

Turning Mistakes into Opportunities

Mistakes are often seen as adverse events, but they are incredibly valuable if approached correctly. Each mistake is an opportunity to learn, grow, and improve. It's a chance to gain new insights and develop a more robust approach to challenges.

How to Turn Mistakes into Learning Experiences:

- **Acknowledge the Error:** Own up to your mistakes. Denial only stunts your growth.

- **Analyze What Went Wrong:** Understand why the mistake happened. What factors contributed to it?

- **Extract Lessons:** Determine what you can learn from the experience. How can you avoid similar mistakes in the future?

- **Apply the Knowledge:** Use the insights gained to make better decisions.

Keep Moving Forward

Resilience, quick problem-solving, and learning from mistakes create a powerful momentum that propels you forward. Progress is not typically a straight line; it's a series of steps forward, setbacks, and recoveries. The key is to keep moving, regardless of the challenges you face.

Tips to Maintain Momentum:

- **Set Clear Goals:** Know where you're headed. Clear objectives provide direction and motivation.

- **Stay Positive:** Maintain a positive outlook, even in adversity. Your attitude can influence your outcomes.

- **Seek Support:** Surround yourself with supportive people who encourage and motivate you.

- **Celebrate Small Wins:** Acknowledge your successes, no matter how small. They build confidence and keep you motivated.

Resilience Across Domains

Resilience isn't just a buzzword; it's a critical skill that helps individuals thrive in various aspects of life, business, and sports. Whether you're an entrepreneur facing market fluctuations, an athlete aiming for a comeback or a student navigating academic challenges, resilience can be your most valuable asset.

Growth Mindset

What is a Growth Mindset?

A growth mindset, popularized by psychologist Carol Dweck, is the belief that abilities and intelligence can be developed through hard work, dedication, and learning from failure. This mindset is crucial for building resilience and encouraging continuous improvement and adaptability.

How Entrepreneurs Benefit

Entrepreneurs with a growth mindset see failures as opportunities to learn and grow. They actively seek feedback, innovate, and pivot their strategies to adapt to changing market conditions. This ability to learn and adapt quickly often sets successful entrepreneurs apart.

Application in Sports

Athletes with a growth mindset outperform those with a fixed mindset. They understand that talent alone isn't enough; hard work and perseverance are key. This mindset allows them to push through setbacks, recover from injuries, and continuously improve their performance.

Importance for Students

A growth mindset is essential for academic success. It encourages students to view challenges as learning opportunities rather than insurmountable obstacles. This mindset fosters a love for learning and builds the resilience to tackle complex subjects or coursework.

Overcoming Setbacks - The Inevitable Hurdles

Setbacks are a part of life, but how you respond to them defines your life. Overcoming setbacks involves:

- Recognizing the issue.

- Devising a plan to address it.

- Maintaining a positive attitude throughout the process.

Entrepreneurs and Setbacks

Entrepreneurs face numerous setbacks, from funding issues to market competition. The key to overcoming these setbacks lies in problem-solving and maintaining a positive outlook. Successful entrepreneurs view setbacks as temporary and solvable, which allows them to keep moving forward.

Athletes and Comebacks

In sports, setbacks like injuries or losses are part of the game. What sets resilient athletes apart is their ability to come back stronger. They use setbacks as fuel to train harder, improve their techniques, and focus on their goals.

Students and Academic Challenges

Students encounter various academic challenges, from failing grades to challenging subjects. Resilient students don't give up; they seek help, adjust their study habits, and stay committed to their academic goals. Overcoming these setbacks not only improves their grades but also builds their character.

Adaptability

Why Adaptability Matters

Adaptability is the ability to adjust to new conditions. In a rapidly changing world, being adaptable is crucial for survival and success in any domain. It allows you to pivot your strategies, learn new skills, and stay relevant.

Entrepreneurs and Market Changes

Markets are volatile, and consumer preferences change rapidly. Adaptable entrepreneurs can quickly pivot their business models, adopt new technologies, and seize emerging opportunities. This adaptability is often the difference between a thriving business and a failure.

Athletes and Changing Conditions

In sports, conditions can change instantly—weather, opponents, or even rules. Adaptable athletes can adjust their strategies and maintain their performance levels regardless of these changes. This ability to adapt quickly makes them more versatile and competitive.

Students and Learning Environments

The educational landscape continually evolves, with new technologies and teaching methods emerging regularly. Adaptable students can easily adjust to different learning environments, whether online or in traditional classrooms. This adaptability enhances their learning experience and prepares them for future challenges.

Achieving Peace of Mind Through Resilience in Life, Business, and Sports

Life Resilience and Mental Health

Resilience is the ability to bounce back from setbacks or difficult situations. In today's fast-paced world, stress and mental health issues are common. Being resilient can help individuals cope with these challenges and maintain their well-being.

Business Resilience in Crisis

In times of crisis, businesses that have built Resilience can quickly adapt to changing market conditions and stay afloat by having contingency plans, diversifying revenue streams, and fostering a culture of innovation within the organization.

Sports Resilience Building

Athletes face numerous challenges on and off the field - injuries, losses, and intense pressure to perform. Those who build resilience can overcome.

Resilience is a multifaceted skill that can be developed through a growth mindset, overcoming setbacks and adaptability. Whether you're an entrepreneur, athlete, or student, these elements of resilience will help you navigate challenges and achieve your goals.

Chapter 38

Risk Management

"Do not go where the path may lead, go instead where there is no path and leave a trail." — **Ralph Waldo Emerson**

This quote by Ralph Waldo Emerson inspires individuals to forge their own unique paths and embrace originality. By venturing into uncharted territories and challenging the status quo, one is more likely to discover new opportunities and drive meaningful change. The pursuit of innovation often requires courage and a willingness to take risks, empowering leaders and creators to blaze trails for others to follow.

Achieving Success through Risk Management in Life, Business, and Sports

Today, the power of management can be the defining factor between triumph and defeat in our ever-changing world. Whether at the helm of a business, in the heat of competition, or steering personal finances, the ability to identify, assess, and mitigate risks is a game-changer. Let's delve into the fundamental principles of risk management and witness how these strategies have empowered individuals to achieve significant success in diverse fields.

Fundamental Principles of Risk Management

1. Identify and Assess Potential Risks and Opportunities

The first step in effective risk management is identifying potential risks and opportunities, which involve understanding the landscape in which you operate and recognizing factors which could impact your objectives. In business, this might mean analyzing market trends and competitor actions. In sports, it could involve assessing the opponent's strengths and weaknesses. In life, this might include evaluating financial options or health outcomes.

2. Develop a Risk Management Plan Tailored to Your Situation

A one-size-fits-all approach rarely works in risk management. A tailored plan that addresses your unique circumstances is essential. This plan should outline the specific risks you face, the potential impact of those risks, and the strategies you will implement to address them.

3. Implement Strategies to Mitigate, Transfer, or Accept Risks

Once you have identified risks and developed a plan, the next step is implementation, which involves strategies to:

- Mitigate risks by reducing their likelihood or impact (e.g., diversifying investments).

- Transfer risks by outsourcing or insuring against them (e.g., purchasing insurance).

- Accept risks when the potential benefits outweigh the downsides (e.g., entering a new market).

4. Continuously Monitor and Review Your Risk Management Plan for Effectiveness

Risk management is not a one-time task. Continuous monitoring and regular reviews are essential to ensure the effectiveness of your strategies. Adjustments may be necessary as new risks emerge or circumstances change.

5. Foster a Culture of Risk Awareness and Responsibility

Creating a culture where everyone is aware of and responsible for managing risks is critical, as well as educating your team or organization about risk management principles and encouraging proactive risk assessment and reporting.

Real-Life Examples of Risk Management Success

Apple's Diversification Strategy

Apple's decision to diversify its product portfolio beyond computers, including the iPhone and iPad, is a textbook example of successful risk management in business. By expanding into new markets, Apple mitigated the risk of stagnating sales and dependency on a single product line. This strategic move spurred growth and secured Apple's position as a leader in consumer electronics.

The New England Patriots Team Building

The New England Patriots have demonstrated exceptional risk management in sports through strategic player acquisitions and draft picks. By continuously evaluating and adapting their team composition, the Patriots have mitigated risks associated with aging players or underperformance. This approach has kept them consistently competitive, leading to numerous championships.

Diversifying an Investment Portfolio

In personal finance, diversifying an investment portfolio is a practical example of risk management. Individuals can protect their financial health by spreading investments across different asset classes (e.g., stocks, bonds, real estate). A downturn in one investment is less likely to impact the overall portfolio significantly, thus ensuring more excellent financial stability.

Effective risk management is a powerful tool for achieving success in life, business, or sports. You can turn potential threats into opportunities by identifying and assessing risks, developing tailored plans, implementing strategies, and fostering a culture of risk awareness.

Addition Building and Design, Inc. – Los Angeles, CA

This successful Residential Design Build firm assesses risk with all clients before purchasing a property, building a new home or major renovation.

Many factors come into play:

- How long will you live at the property
- What is the buildable living area per building code in the area
- What is the square foot dollar value
- What will be the investment return in five years

Risk Management Success and Peace of Mind in Life, Business, and Sports

Achieving success through risk management not only enhances performance but also contributes to peace of mind across various domains. Individuals can navigate uncertainties by establishing contingency plans and setting realistic goals, allowing them to approach challenges confidently. In business, successful leaders maintain a proactive stance towards risk, fostering environments where innovation thrives without compromising stability. This balance cultivates trust among stakeholders and employees, sustaining growth and resilience. Similarly, in sports, teams that effectively manage risks—through thorough preparation and adaptable strategies—often experience lower anxiety levels among players, enabling them to perform at their peak without the overwhelming fear of failure. Ultimately, the synergy between effective risk management and peace of mind creates a foundation for continual achievement and fulfillment.

Chapter 39

Reputation Matters

"Reputation is an outcome; but it is also a point of influence in itself, and a point of influence that can shape your company or your future." — **Carly Fiorina**

The former CEO of Hewlett-Packard, Carly Fiorina underscores the critical role of reputation in both defining and influencing success. She emphasizes that while reputation is a result of one's actions and decisions, it also serves as a powerful tool that can open doors to future opportunities.

When building your reputation, here are three essential rules:

1. Use your BEST workers and use the BEST materials.

2. Make sure you treat your first five customers above and beyond ordinary, as you will immediately have 5-10 salespeople telling all their family, friends, and co-workers how amazing this new company is.

3. Marketing materials must be 1st class-looking, including good paper stock, quality printing, and great photos.

In life, business, and sports, reputation is everything. The invisible currency holds immense power over the doors that open for you, the opportunities you seize, and the relationships you build. Here's why reputation must be considered and how it shapes individuals' and organizations' paths.

The Cornerstone of Trust

Your reputation serves as a foundation for trust in personal and professional relationships. It measures your integrity and reliability, influencing how others perceive and interact with you. A solid reputation can make people more willing to engage with you, collaborate, and support your endeavors.

Opening Doors and Creating Opportunities

A good reputation can significantly enhance your prospects in both business and personal life. It acts as a magnet, drawing customers, investors, and top talent to you. Take Apple Inc., for example. Known for its innovative products and unwavering commitment to quality, Apple has built a strong global reputation that attracts loyal customers and investors.

Similarly, Oprah Winfrey's consistent philanthropy work and empowering messages have established a positive personal brand, opening doors across various industries. Her reputation for authenticity and kindness has made her a trusted media figure.

A Measure of Integrity and Reliability

Your reputation reflects your integrity and reliability. In business, these qualities are paramount. A positive reputation can increase customer loyalty, while a tarnished image can result in significant losses. For example, the Enron Corporation was once a leading energy company, but a series of accounting scandals shattered its reputation, leading to bankruptcy and severe legal repercussions.

Attracting Customers, Investors, and Talent

A good business reputation is a powerful asset. It can attract not only customers but also investors and top-tier talent. Companies known for their ethical practices, transparency, and effective communication stand out in a crowded market. They have become the preferred choice for consumers and professionals alike.

Influence in the Sports World

In sports, reputation can make or break careers. Athletes with a positive image enjoy numerous benefits, including sponsorship deals, fan support, and career longevity. LeBron James, for example, transcends his immense talent with a reputation for community involvement and leadership on and off the court. His positive image has secured him endorsement deals and respect across the sports world.

On the flip side, a damaged reputation can have dire consequences. Despite being one of the most successful golfers, Tiger Woods's career was significantly impacted by personal life scandals, including sponsorship losses, which damaged his public image.

The Digital Age and Reputation Management

The digital age has technologically amplified the importance of reputation management. Online reviews and social media play significant roles in shaping public perception. One misstep can quickly go viral, causing long-lasting damage. United Airlines is a prime example. The mishandling of a customer service incident led to a viral video, resulting in a significant dip in the airline's reputation and a subsequent loss in stock value.

Building and Maintaining a Positive Reputation

Building and maintaining a positive reputation requires consistent ethical behavior, transparency, and effective communication. It is an ongoing effort that demands attention and care. Here are some key strategies:

- **Act Ethically**: Consistently demonstrate ethical behavior in all your actions. Integrity speaks volumes.

- **Be Transparent**: Open communication and honesty build trust. Share both successes and challenges with your audience.

- **Engage Effectively**: Listen to your audience and respond to their feedback. Engagement shows that you value their opinions and are committed to improvement.

Achieving Peace of Mind Through a Successful Reputation in Life, Business and Sports

In the business world, a solid reputation attracts customers, partners, and opportunities, alleviating the stress associated with uncertainty and competition.

Similarly, in sports, athletes with a good reputation often enjoy better sponsorship deals and fan support, contributing to a sense of security and motivation. By prioritizing ethical practices and communication, we can cultivate a reputation that enhances our external interactions and contributes to our inner peace, empowering us to face life's challenges with resilience.

Reputation is not just a reflection of who we are but a critical asset that influences every aspect of our lives. A positive reputation can open doors, create opportunities, and establish trust in business, sports, or personal relationships. Conversely, a damaged reputation can lead to significant setbacks and losses.

Remember, building and maintaining a positive reputation is an ongoing effort. It requires consistent ethical behavior, transparency, and effective communication. If you're ready to take your reputation to the next level, consider booking a consultation with one of our experts. We can ensure that your reputation works for you, not against you.

Chapter 40

Building a Winning Culture

"Good teams become great ones when the members trust each other enough to surrender the 'me' for the 'we'." — Phil Jackson

This quote by the legendary basketball coach, Phil Jackson, underlines the strategic importance of teamwork and trust within a sports team. It suggests that success is achieved not just through individual talent, but also through the unified effort and commitment to the collective goal.

Creating a winning culture in any organization is no small feat. It requires a shared vision, a commitment to core values, and the implementation of critical initiatives that foster growth, collaboration, and resilience.

Here's how you can cultivate a winning culture in your organization:

Core Values that Define Our Culture

At the heart of our winning culture are six core values that not only guide everything we do but also serve as the bedrock of our organizational identity:

- **Honesty**: We believe in transparency and truthfulness in all interactions, which are trust and the foundation for solid relationships.

- **Communication**: Clear and open communication is essential for collaboration and success. We ensure everyone is on the same page and feels heard.

- **Teamwork**: Build a Culture where people depend on people.

- **Hard Work**: There are no shortcuts to success. Dedication and effort are crucial to achieving our goals.

- **Empathy** and **Compassion**: We care about each other. Understanding and supporting one another through challenges creates a supportive and nurturing work environment.

Success Stories Illustrating Our Winning Culture

Exceptional Teamwork and Communication

One of our most remarkable success stories involves a complex project completed ahead of schedule. The project's success was a direct result of the exceptional teamwork and communication among team members. Daily stand-up meetings, instant message updates, and collaborative tools ensured everyone was aligned and could address any issues promptly. This example vividly demonstrates our values of teamwork and communication in action.

Going Above and Beyond with Empathy and Compassion

Another standout story involves an employee who went above and beyond to support a colleague during a difficult personal time. The employee covered their colleague's responsibilities and offered emotional support. This act of kindness reflected our core values of empathy and compassion, showing that we are more than just co-workers, we are a family.

Overcoming Challenges with Hard Work and Resilience

Lastly, we faced a project that encountered significant challenges, including tight deadlines and unexpected obstacles. Through sheer hard work and resilience, the team completed the project. This story highlights our organization's commitment to both hard work and determination, proving we can overcome challenges.

Key Initiatives to Foster a Winning Culture

To continuously build and nurture our winning culture, we have implemented several key initiatives:

1. Learning and Development Programs

We offer regular training sessions and workshops to help employees develop their skills and stay updated with industry trends. These steps enhance individual capabilities and ensure our team remains competitive and innovative.

2. Wellness Programs

Understanding the importance of mental and physical well-being, we have wellness programs that include mindfulness sessions, fitness challenges, and mental health resources. Achieving peace of mind is crucial for maintaining a positive and productive work environment.

3. Recognition and Rewards

Acknowledging hard work and achievements is vital. We have a robust recognition program where employees are rewarded for their contributions. Rewards boost morale and motivate everyone to strive for excellence.

4. Community Engagement

We encourage our team to participate in community service and volunteer work. This initiative helps those in need and fosters a sense of empathy and compassion within our organization.

5. Open-Door Policy

Our leadership maintains an open-door policy ensuring employees feel comfortable sharing their ideas, concerns, and Feedback, promoting a culture of transparency and continuous improvement.

Make it Happen

Building a winning culture is an ongoing process that requires dedication, consistency, and a commitment to core values. We foster honesty, communication, teamwork, hard work, empathy, and compassion to create an environment where everyone can thrive.

If you're interested in learning more about how we cultivate this culture or want to join us on this journey, don't hesitate to reach out. Together, we can achieve great things.

Achieving Peace of Mind in Building a Winning Culture in Life, Business, and Sports

Achieving peace of mind is essential across various domains, including life, business, and sports.

In a thriving organizational culture, a foundation of trust and open communication enables employees to express themselves freely, fostering a positive atmosphere, translating to higher engagement levels, innovative thinking, and reduced workplace stress in business.

Similarly, peace of mind in sports allows athletes to focus on their performance, build resilience, and collaborate effectively with teammates. By prioritizing mental well-being and creating a culture that supports emotional health, organizations can cultivate an environment where individuals thrive, ultimately leading to collective success and fulfillment.

Chapter 41

Derailments

"It's not whether you get knocked down; it's whether you get up."
— **Vince Lombardi**

Legendary football coach Vince Lombardi stresses the importance of resilience in overcoming life's derailments. His powerful words remind us that the true measure of success lies in our ability to rise and try again after setbacks.

Setbacks are an inevitable part of any significant endeavor. Whether you're an entrepreneur, athlete, student, or individual in any field, life's challenges can sometimes derail you from your path. But remember, getting back on track is essential. Don't quit—use these setbacks as stepping stones to more significant achievements.

Keys to Surviving Derailments:

1. Stop making excuses and blaming others for problems.

2. Solve the problem and solve the problem quickly—this is the key to surpassing your opponent or co-worker.

3. Put together the plan toward success.

4. Remember your lesson to minimize the chances of this derailment ever happening again.

Let's explore some powerful stories of resilience and learn how to overcome setbacks in various fields, from business and sports to personal relationships and academic pursuits.

Steve Jobs and His Journey Back to Apple

Steve Jobs' story is one of the most iconic in the tech industry. In 1985, Jobs was ousted from Apple, the company he co-founded, which would have been the end for many, but not for Jobs. He founded NeXT and acquired Pixar, which revolutionized the animation industry. In 1996, Apple acquired NeXT, leading to Jobs' return. His comeback heralded groundbreaking innovations like the iMac, iPod, iPhone, and iPad. Job's story teaches us that setbacks can lead to even greater success.

Michael Jordan's High School Cut

Before becoming one of the greatest basketball players ever, Michael Jordan faced a significant setback when he was cut from his high school basketball team. Rather than giving up, Jordan used this experience as fuel to improve his game. His relentless work ethic and determination made him a six-time NBA champion and a global sports icon. Jordan's story reminds us that setbacks are temporary, but the drive to succeed can last a lifetime.

J.K. Rowling's Road to Success

J.K. Rowling, the author of the beloved **Harry Potter** series, faced numerous rejections before finding success. Living in relative poverty, she submitted her manuscript to multiple publishers, only to receive rejection after rejection. However, her persistence paid off when Bloomsbury finally published her book. Today, Rowling is one of the most successful authors in history, with millions of fans worldwide. Her story emphasizes the importance of perseverance and believing in your vision, even in the face of repeated failures.

Local Entrepreneur's Comeback from Bankruptcy

Near home, we have the inspiring story of a local entrepreneur who faced bankruptcy but refused to give up. His resilience and refusal to be defeated by the setback is a testament to the human spirit. After his business collapsed, he analyzed what went wrong and adapted his strategies. Through resilience and innovation, he rebuilt his business, which is thriving more than ever. His story shows that even in the darkest times, there's always a way to turn things around with the right mindset and actions.

Strategies for Overcoming Setbacks

1. Acknowledge and Accept

The first step in overcoming setbacks is to acknowledge and accept them. Denial can only prolong the process. Admitting that something went wrong allows you to start working on a solution.

2. Learn from the Experience

Each setback holds valuable lessons. Reflect on what went wrong and why. This self-awareness can prevent similar issues in the future and contribute to personal and professional growth.

3. Stay Positive and Resilient

Maintaining a positive outlook is crucial. Remember, setbacks are temporary. Resilience is about bouncing back more robust and more determined. Keep your eyes on your goals and stay motivated.

4. Seek Support

Don't hesitate to seek support from friends, family, mentors, or professionals. The support offered may include nuggets of valuable advice, encouragement, and a fresh perspective to help you overcome challenges. Remember, you're not alone in this journey.

5. Adapt and Innovate

Sometimes, overcoming a setback requires adapting and innovating. Be open to change and willing to try new approaches. Remember, flexibility is not a sign of weakness, but strength. It can lead to discovering better paths forward and empower you to overcome any obstacle.

6. Take Action

Ultimately, overcoming setbacks involves taking concrete actions. Develop a plan, set small, achievable goals, and start working towards them. No matter how small, each action brings you closer to getting back on track.

Achieving Peace of Mind when Derailed in Life, Business, and Sports, and Rebounding Successfully

Experiencing derailment in life, business, or sports is a common challenge everyone faces. Feeling off course can be disheartening, whether a personal crisis, a failed project, or a losing streak.

However, the *ability to rebound successfully* lies in your response to these setbacks. It starts with a mindset shift—viewing obstacles not as permanent roadblocks but as opportunities for growth.

Applying the strategies outlined previously, you can build resilience and develop the skills necessary to navigate adversity.

In life, maintaining a good work-life balance and setting realistic expectations can help mitigate feelings of being overwhelmed. Analyzing market changes and customer feedback allows for better adaptation and strategy realignment in business.

For athletes, focusing on training, refining techniques, and maintaining a positive mental attitude can turn a challenging period into a springboard for success.

Ultimately, embracing setbacks as part of the journey fosters a stronger, more adaptable self, better equipped to handle future challenges.

Setbacks are not the end of the road but rather a detour that can lead to greater heights. Whether you're an entrepreneur, athlete, or student, remember that resilience, perseverance, and a positive mindset are crucial to overcoming any obstacle. Take inspiration from the stories of Steve Jobs, Michael Jordan, J.K. Rowling, and countless others who turned their setbacks into comebacks. Keep pushing forward, stay focused on your goals, and don't quit. Now, it's your turn. Apply these strategies in your own life and turn your setbacks into stepping stones for success.

Chapter 42

Exceeding Expectations

"The only place where success comes before work is in the dictionary." — Vidal Sassoon

Entrepreneur Vidal Sassoon reminds us that hard work is a prerequisite for achieving success, emphasizing the importance of effort and dedication to exceed customers' expectations.

Success in life, business, and sports is driven by a blend of hard work, resilience, and strategic thinking. Whether you're an entrepreneur aiming to exceed client expectations or an athlete striving for peak performance, the principles of excellence are remarkably consistent. This guide explores proven ways to excel in these domains, ensuring sustainable and authentic growth without overpromising.

Proven Ways to Exceed Clients' and Athletes' Expectations

Set Realistic Goals and Benchmarks

For Entrepreneurs:

- **Understanding Client Needs** is the cornerstone of your business. Conduct thorough market research and interview clients to understand their pain points and expectations. For Athletes, Assessing Your Current Level is the first step towards improvement. Understand your strengths and weaknesses through self-assessment and coach feedback.

- **Set Clear Milestones**: Break down projects into manageable tasks with clear deadlines. This helps you track progress and make necessary adjustments.

- **Communicate Transparently**: Keep clients informed about project status, potential delays, and challenges. Transparency builds trust and manages expectations.

For Athletes:

- **Assess Your Current Level**: Understand your strengths and weaknesses through self-assessment and coach feedback.

- **Create a Training Plan**: Develop a structured plan with short-term and long-term goals. Make sure it's realistic and achievable to avoid burnout.

- **Monitor Progress**: Track your progress regularly and adjust your training regimen as needed. Celebrate small victories to stay motivated.

Continuous Learning and Adaptation

For Entrepreneurs:

- **Stay Informed**: Keep up with industry trends, competitor strategies, and technological advancements. Knowledge is power.

- **Seek Feedback**: Regularly ask for feedback from clients and team members. Use this feedback to improve your services and processes.

- **Invest in Skill Development**: Attend workshops, webinars, and courses to enhance your skills and stay competitive.

For Athletes:

- **Analyze Competitions**: Study your performances and those of your competitors. Identify areas for improvement and strategies that can give you an edge.

- **Adapt Training Techniques**: Be open to incorporating new training methods, diets, and recovery techniques. Flexibility can lead to breakthroughs.

- **Mental Conditioning**: Work on mental toughness and resilience. Practices like visualization and mindfulness can significantly improve performance under pressure.

Build Strong Relationships

For Entrepreneurs:

- **Network**: Build a strong professional network by attending industry events, joining relevant online groups, and connecting with thought leaders.

- **Client Engagement**: Go beyond transactional relationships. Show genuine interest in your client's success and find ways to add value to their business.

- **Team Culture**: Foster a positive and collaborative work environment. A motivated and cohesive team is more likely to exceed client expectations.

For Athletes:

- **Team Dynamics**: If you're part of a team sport, build strong relationships with your teammates. Trust and coordination are crucial to team success.
- **Coaching Relationships**: Maintain open and honest communication with your coaches. Their guidance is crucial to your development.

- **Community Engagement**: Engage with fans and the sporting community. Support from a loyal fan base can be incredibly motivating.

Maintain Consistency and Quality

For Entrepreneurs:

- **Standardize Processes**: Develop and adhere to standardized processes to ensure consistent service quality, making scaling easier.

- **Quality Assurance**: Implement regular quality checks and audits. This will help maintain high standards and rectify issues promptly.

- **Deliver Value**: Focus on adding real value to your clients. Whether through innovative solutions, exceptional service, or personalized attention, consistently strive to exceed their expectations.

For Athletes:

- **Stick to Routine**: Consistency in training, nutrition, and rest is crucial to maintaining peak performance.

- **Focus on Fundamentals**: Master the basics before moving on to advanced techniques. Strong fundamentals form the foundation for excellence.

- **Commitment to Excellence**: Always give your best effort in training or competition. Consistent effort leads to consistent results.

Balance and Well-Being

For Entrepreneurs and Athletes:

- **Work-Life Balance**: Avoid burnout by balancing work (or training) and personal life. Take time to rest and recharge.

- **Holistic Health**: Pay attention to both physical and mental health. Regular exercise, a balanced diet, and sufficient sleep are non-negotiables.

- **Mindfulness Practices**: Incorporate practices like meditation, yoga, or even simple breathing exercises to manage stress and enhance focus.

Achieving Peace of Mind when Exceeding Expectations in Life, Business, and Sports

Achieving success in any endeavor often brings about a profound sense of fulfillment and peace of mind.

For entrepreneurs, exceeding client expectations bolsters reputation and fosters trust and loyalty, creating a solid foundation for future growth.

In sports, consistently surpassing personal records or team goals engenders deep satisfaction, reinforcing the belief in one's abilities and commitment to continuous improvement.

Furthermore, embracing a balanced approach to life, incorporating well-being and mindfulness, can enhance focus and performance, making the journey towards greatness more enjoyable. Ultimately, the harmony between striving for excellence and cultivating inner peace is crucial for long-term success and happiness.

Exceeding expectations, whether in business or sports, requires a strategic approach, continuous improvement, and a commitment to excellence. Remember, you can achieve remarkable success without overpromising by setting realistic goals, fostering strong relationships, maintaining consistency, and prioritizing well-being.

Chapter 43

Mastering Delegation

"Great things in business are never done by one person; they're done by a team of people." — **Steve Jobs**

Steve Jobs, the visionary co-founder of Apple Inc., attributed much of his success to the exceptional teams he worked with. His statement reiterates the importance of teamwork in driving innovation and achieving groundbreaking results in any professional setting.

Delegating is vital for great leaders in life, business, and sports. It enhances productivity, fosters team growth, and allows leaders to focus on high-impact tasks. Let's explore the key points to delegate tasks effectively and how they can transform your leadership approach.

Why Delegation Matters

Achieving success through delegation is a powerful strategy that can be applied across various domains such as life, business, and sports. Here's how delegation can enhance performance and lead to success in each area:

Life

- **Time Management**: Delegating tasks such as household chores or planning events can free up time for more important activities, like pursuing hobbies or spending time with loved ones.
- **Skill Utilization**: Recognizing and utilizing the strengths of others can lead to better outcomes. For instance, if someone is

a great cook, delegating meal preparation can enhance family gatherings.

- **Stress Reduction**: Sharing responsibilities can alleviate stress, contributing to mental well-being and improved relationships.

Business

- **Increased Efficiency**: Delegating tasks to team members allows leaders to focus on strategic planning and decision-making, ultimately leading to better productivity.

- **Empowerment and Growth**: When employees are given responsibility, they feel valued and are more likely to develop their skills, fostering a culture of growth within the organization.

- **Enhanced Innovation**: Diverse perspectives from team members can lead to innovative solutions. Delegating encourages collaboration and idea-sharing.

Sports

- **Team Dynamics**: In team sports, successful delegation involves recognizing each player's strengths and assigning roles accordingly. This successfully fosters teamwork and enhances performance.

- **Coaching**: Coaches who delegate responsibilities, such as training specific skills or managing game strategies, can focus on overall team development and tactical adjustments.

- **Mental Focus**: Athletes can concentrate on their performance rather than getting bogged down by every minor detail, leading to better outcomes during competitions.

Critical Tips for Effective Delegation

1. Choose the Right People

Selecting the right individuals for the task is crucial. Here's what to consider:

- **Background Check**: Understand their experience and skills to ensure they are suited for the task.

- **Intelligence**: Are they intelligent and capable of handling complex tasks?

- **Accountability**: Can they take ownership and deliver results?

- **Team Players**: Are they able to collaborate and work well with others?

- **Drive**: Do they show enthusiasm and motivation to complete the task?

2. Encourage Feedback

Create an environment where team members feel comfortable providing feedback, which refines the process and ensures everyone is on the same page.

3. Build Trust

Trust is the foundation of effective delegation. Show confidence in your team's abilities and avoid micromanaging. This will not only build their confidence but also foster a sense of security and connection in the team, leading to a more productive working environment.

4. Identify Work to Delegate

Not all tasks need to be handled by you. Identify functions that will be delegated without compromising quality or efficiency.

5. Delegate Gradually

Start with small tasks and gradually increase the complexity as your team members grow more confident and capable.

6. Provide Clarity on Task Instructions

Clear instructions are essential for successful delegation. Outline the task, your expectations, and any necessary guidelines.

7. Set Deadlines

Provide a realistic deadline for task completion. This helps manage time effectively, keeps everyone on track, and gives a sense of control over the workflow.

Achieving Peace of Mind in Delegating Successfully in Life, Business, and Sports

In all areas of life, effective delegation is about recognizing the strengths of others and distributing tasks accordingly. By doing so, individuals can achieve greater success, foster collaboration, and create a more balanced approach to challenges.

Embrace delegation as a key component of your strategy for success, whether in personal endeavors, professional environments, or athletic pursuits.

Delegating is crucial for achieving peace of mind in personal life, business, or sports. By entrusting others with responsibilities, individuals can focus on their core priorities and reduce stress.

In business, delegation fosters collaboration and allows leaders to tap into the diverse skills of their team, ultimately enhancing productivity and innovation.

In sports, delegates can streamline strategies and training, ensuring everyone plays to their strengths.

Achieving peace of mind comes from clear communication, establishing Trust, and ensuring that expectations are understood, allowing for a harmonious and prosperous environment where all contributions are valued.

Chapter 44

How to Identify What the Missing Pieces Are in Your Life, Business, or Team

"Don't be afraid to give up the good to go for the great." — **John D. Rockefeller**

Business magnate John D. Rockefeller encourages taking calculated risks to achieve outstanding success, advocating for the pursuit of greatness over complacency with mediocrity.

Identifying the missing pieces in various aspects of life, business, and sports can lead to significant personal growth and improvement. Here's a structured approach to help you pinpoint these areas:

Life

1. Self-Reflection:

- What are your core values?
- Are you achieving your personal goals?

2. Relationships:

- Are you satisfied with your social connections?
- Do you have a support system?

3. Health:

- Are you maintaining physical and mental well-being?
- Are there habits you want to change?

4. Work-Life Balance:

- Are you spending enough time on hobbies and relaxation?
- Do you feel overwhelmed or stressed?

Business

1. Vision and Goals:

- Are your business goals clearly defined?
- Do you have a long-term vision?

2. Market Understanding:

- Do you know your target audience well?
- Are you keeping up with industry trends?

3. Resources:

- Do you have the necessary tools and technology?
- Are you leveraging your team's strengths effectively?

4. Financial Health:

- Are you tracking your finances accurately?
- Do you have a budget or financial plan?

In today's competitive market, the power to understand and bridge your company's gaps is a key to achieving profitability and sustained growth. Whether the challenges are related to profitability, generating more leads, increasing staff productivity, or managing production costs, identifying these missing pieces is the first step towards formulating effective strategies. Below, we'll guide you through a comprehensive approach to identifying and addressing these gaps, putting you in the driver's seat of your company's success.

Sports

1. Skill Development:

- Are there specific skills you need to improve?
- Are you practicing consistently?

2. Mental Toughness:

- How do you handle pressure and setbacks?
- Are you focused and motivated?

3. Coaching and Support:

- Do you have access to a coach or mentor?
- Are you part of a team or community for support?

4. Injury Prevention:

- Are you taking care of your body?
- Do you have a recovery plan?

Action Plan

1. Set Clear Goals: Define what you want to achieve in each area.

2. Seek Feedback: Talk to trusted friends, colleagues, or mentors for insights.

3. Create a Plan: Develop actionable steps to address the identified gaps.

4. Monitor Progress: Regularly review your progress and adjust your plan as needed.

By systematically assessing these areas, you can uncover the missing pieces and create a roadmap for improvement.

Assessing Current Challenges

Profitability Concerns

- **Analyze Financial Statements**: Start by thoroughly reviewing your income statements, balance sheets, and cash flow statements. Look for trends and anomalies that indicate inefficiencies or unnecessary expenses.

- **For instance, if you're a manufacturing company, you can** break down your costs into raw materials, labor, and overheads. Are there any areas where costs can be reduced without compromising quality? For example, you might find that by renegotiating with your suppliers, you can reduce your raw material costs without affecting the quality of your products.

Need More Leads to Increase Sales

- **Evaluate Marketing Effectiveness**: Audit your current marketing strategies and campaigns. Which channels are providing the best ROI? Are there any underperforming tactics that need to be reconsidered or optimized?

- **Customer Feedback**: Gather feedback from your existing customers to understand their needs and preferences. This can help tailor your marketing efforts to attract similar leads.

More Productivity from Staff

- **Performance Metrics**: Implement and track KPIs to measure staff productivity. Identify areas where employees may need additional support or training.

- **Employee Engagement**: Conduct surveys or interviews to gauge employee satisfaction and identify any barriers to productivity. Engaged employees are often more productive and committed.

Cost to Produce Products

- **Supply Chain Efficiency**: Review your supply chain to identify bottlenecks or inefficiencies. Are there opportunities to negotiate better terms with suppliers or streamline logistics?

- **Production Process**: Analyze your production processes for waste or redundancy. Implementing lean manufacturing techniques can often lead to significant cost savings.

Aligning with Company Goals- Life, Business, and Sports

Profitability

- **Break-Even Analysis**: Understand your break-even point and strive to exceed it. Use this as a benchmark for setting financial goals and making informed decisions.

- **Profit Margins**: Focus on products or services with higher profit margins. If they do not contribute positively to the bottom line, consider phasing out low-margin offerings.

Enough Leads to Close Jobs

- **Lead Generation Strategies**: Develop targeted campaigns based on customer personas. Utilize SEO, content marketing, social media, and PPC advertising to reach a broader audience.

- **Sales Funnel Optimization**: Ensure that your sales funnel is efficient and effective. Identify any stages where leads drop off and implement strategies to nurture them through conversion.

Leveraging Available Resources

Skilled and Experienced Staff

- **Training Programs**: Invest in ongoing training and development to keep skills sharp and relevant.

- **Mentorship and Collaboration**: Foster a mentorship and collaboration culture to maximize your experienced staff's potential.

Marketing and Sales Team

- **Cross-functional collaboration**: Encourage collaboration between marketing and sales teams to ensure alignment and maximize lead generation and conversion efforts.

- **Innovative Tools**: Equip your teams with the latest marketing and sales tools to enhance efficiency and effectiveness.

Existing Client Base and Referrals

- **Customer Loyalty Programs**: Implement loyalty programs to retain existing clients and encourage repeat business.

- **Referral Incentives**: Offer incentives for referrals from satisfied customers and industry colleagues.

Financial Resources for Investment

- **Strategic Investments**: Make sure to allocate your financial resources strategically to areas that promise the highest return on investment.

- **Risk Management**: Diversify investments to mitigate risks and ensure long-term financial stability.

Access to Technology and Industry Tools

- **Tech Upgrades**: Regularly update and maintain your technology stack to stay competitive and efficient.

- **Data Analytics**: Utilize data analytics tools to gain insights into business performance and inform decision-making.

Established Supply Chain and Production Facilities

- **Supplier Relationships**: Maintain strong relationships with suppliers to ensure quality and reliability.

- **Process Improvement**: Continuously seek ways to improve production processes and reduce costs.

Achieving Peace of Mind by Identifying Weaknesses in Life, Business, and Sports

By identifying weaknesses, individuals can begin the journey of personal growth and improvement.

In life, recognizing one's weaknesses involves honest introspection and a willingness to accept areas that require development. This might include aspects such as poor time management, difficulty in communication, or lack of self-discipline. In the business realm, identifying weaknesses could relate to skills gaps, such as lack of technical expertise or ineffective leadership abilities. Acknowledging these areas allows professionals to seek training, mentorship, or further education to enhance their capabilities.

In sports, recognizing weaknesses might include physical limitations, lack of strategy, or mental barriers that hinder performance. Once identified, athletes can work with coaches to tailor their training regimes or adopt mental techniques to strengthen these areas. By understanding and confronting these weaknesses, individuals can transform them into strengths, paving the way for greater success and achievement across all aspects of their lives.

Identifying and addressing the missing pieces in your company requires a strategic and systematic approach.

By assessing current challenges, aligning with company goals, and leveraging available resources, you can pave the way for increased profitability, more leads, and improved productivity. Remember, in the ever-changing business landscape, the ability to adapt and continuously improve is as crucial as identifying the gaps.

By actively identifying and addressing weaknesses in these areas, you can foster a greater sense of control and peace of mind.

Regularly revisiting these strategies will help you adapt and grow, ultimately leading to a more balanced and fulfilling life.

Chapter 45

Clear Vision

"Life is like riding a bicycle. To keep your balance, you must keep moving." — **Albert Einstein**

Albert Einstein, renowned physicist, uses the metaphor of cycling to convey the necessity of forward momentum in overcoming life's obstacles to maintain your focus on the vision.

His advice resonates with the idea that continuous effort and adaptability are keys to maintaining equilibrium through life's ups and downs.

Vision for Success in Life, Business, and Sports

Success is often defined in myriad ways, but to me, success is peace of mind, knowing I have done my best for the family, business, team and myself. It's about achieving a delicate balance between personal fulfillment and professional excellence. This Vision is rooted in clear goals, mindful of the challenges ahead, and steadfast in pursuing continuous growth. Remember, it's okay to struggle with balance-*it's a journey we're all on.*

Goals for Success

Life

My primary goal in life is to maintain a healthy work-life balance. This means being present for my family and friends while also dedicating time to personal growth and fulfillment. Whether through hobbies, learning new skills, or simply taking time for self-care, I strive to nourish my mind, body, and soul.

Business

My business ambition is to lead a team that meets and exceeds targets, which involves fostering a positive and inclusive work environment where every team member feels valued and motivated. By cultivating a culture of collaboration and innovation, we can achieve remarkable success and make a meaningful impact in our industry.

Sports

Regarding sports, my objective is to reach peak physical and mental condition, meaning rigorous training, disciplined nutrition, and a strong mental focus. I aim to perform at my best in every game or competition, pushing my limits and striving for excellence.

Anticipated Challenges

Work-Life Balance

One of the most significant challenges is balancing personal and professional commitments. The risk of burnout is accurate, requiring a conscious effort to ensure neither area suffers. For instance, prioritizing tasks can involve creating a daily to-do list and sticking to it, setting boundaries can mean not checking work emails after a certain time in the evening, and taking regular breaks can be as simple as going for a walk during lunch. These are essential to manage this balance.

Self-Doubt and Motivation

Self-doubt and maintaining motivation during tough times can be challenging in business and sports. But remember, setbacks are part of the journey. Building a solid support network and practicing resilience can help you overcome these obstacles. You are capable of overcoming these challenges.

Competition and Market Trends

Navigating the competitive landscape and unpredictable market trends in business is another challenge. Staying agile, continuously learning and adapting to change are vital to staying ahead. It's about being proactive rather than reactive.

Physical Limitations

Managing injuries or physical limitations affecting sports performance is a constant concern. Preventive care, proper training, and listening to one's body are critical to minimizing risks and ensuring longevity in sports.

Continuous Learning

To stay relevant, it is essential to ensure continuous learning and improvement in all aspects of life, business, and sports. This involves seeking feedback from mentors or peers, investing in education through courses or workshops, and being open to new experiences and perspectives. Continuous learning is not just about acquiring new knowledge, but also about adapting to change and evolving with the times. It's about being proactive rather than reactive.

Negativity

Negativity from people who do not want to see me succeed is a challenge that cannot be ignored. But remember, staying true to your values and surrounding yourself with supportive individuals who uplift and inspire you is key. Let their support inspire you to keep pushing forward.

Achieving Peace of Mind in My Vision for Success in Business, Life, and Sports

Achieving peace of mind in my Vision for success requires a clear vision of mind, body, and spirit that integrates personal well-being with professional aspirations. It starts with cultivating a clear vision that aligns with my values and goals, allowing me to focus on what truly matters.

Embracing mindfulness practices, such as meditation and reflection, can help manage stress and enhance clarity. Additionally, setting realistic expectations and celebrating small achievements fosters a positive mindset.

By balancing ambition with self-compassion, I can navigate challenges resiliently and maintain the inner peace necessary for sustainable success in business, life, and sports.

Chapter 46

Time Management

"Time is the scarcest resource and unless it is managed nothing else can be managed." - Peter Drucker

"Balance is not something you find, it's something you create." — Jana Kingsford

Entrepreneur Jana Kingsford reminds us that balance is an active pursuit, requiring intentional effort and creativity to design a life that aligns with one's values and aspirations.

1. Time Management in Life

Set Clear Goals

- **Specific**: Clearly define your goal.
- **Measurable**: Identify how you will measure progress.
- **Achievable**: Ensure the goal is realistic.
- **Relevant**: Align with your values and long-term objectives.
- **Time-bound**: Set a deadline.

Prioritize Tasks

- **Urgent and Important**: Do these tasks first.
- **Important but Not Urgent**: Schedule these tasks.
- **Urgent but Not Important**: Delegate if possible.
- **Neither Urgent nor Important**: Consider dropping these tasks.

Create a Daily Schedule:

- Plan your day the night before.
- Allocate specific time blocks for tasks.
- Stick to your schedule as closely as possible.

Limit Distractions:

- Identify common distractions (e.g., phone, social media).
- Create a workspace that minimizes interruptions.

Review and Reflect:

- Regularly assess how you spend your time (weekly or monthly).
- Adjust your strategies based on what is working and what isn't.

2. Time Management in Business

Use Project Management Tools:

- Tools like **Day – Timer, Trello, Asana,** or **Monday.com** can help you organize tasks and deadlines.

Delegate Effectively:

- Assign tasks based on team members' strengths.
- Trust your team to handle their responsibilities.

Set Meeting Protocols:

- Keep meetings short and focused.
- Prepare a clear agenda and stick to it.

Avoid Multitasking:

- Focus on one task at a time to improve efficiency and quality.

Conduct Regular Reviews:

- Assess project progress weekly or monthly.
- Make adjustments as necessary to stay on track.

3. Time Management in Sports

Develop a Training Schedule:

- Create a structured plan that includes:
  - **Practice sessions**
  - **Rest days**
  - **Recovery periods**

Set Performance Goals:

- Establish metrics to track improvement (e.g., times, scores).
- Adjust your training based on these metrics.

Prioritize Recovery:

- Ensure time for rest and recovery is built into your training.
- This helps prevent burnout and injuries.

Utilize Time Blocks:

- Break training into focused segments (e.g., skill practice, conditioning).
- This maximizes the effectiveness of each training session.

Incorporate Mental Training:

- Use techniques like visualization and mindfulness to enhance focus and reduce anxiety.

General Tips for All Areas

Use Technology Wisely:

- Leverage apps for task management and reminders.

Practice Self-Discipline:

- Cultivate habits that support your goals.
- Learn to say no to distractions and unproductive activities.

Stay Flexible:

- Be adaptable when plans change.
- Flexibility helps maintain productivity during unexpected situations.

Time Management and Peace of Mind

Effective time management is not just about getting more done; it is a pathway to achieving peace of mind. When you manage your time well, you experience several benefits that contribute to a calmer, more balanced life:

1. **Reduced Stress**: By prioritizing tasks and setting realistic deadlines, you minimize the last-minute rush and the anxiety that comes with it. Knowing you have a plan in place allows you to approach challenges with confidence.

2. **Increased Control**: Time management gives you a sense of control over your day. When you allocate time for tasks, you can better manage your responsibilities, which leads to a

feeling of empowerment and reduces feelings of being overwhelmed.

3. **Enhanced Focus**: With a clear schedule, you can concentrate on one task at a time, which not only improves the quality of your work but also fosters a sense of accomplishment. This focus helps you avoid the mental clutter that often leads to stress.

4. **Better Work-Life Balance**: Effective time management allows you to allocate time for both work and personal activities. By creating boundaries and prioritizing leisure and family time, you enhance your overall well-being and satisfaction in life.

5. **Opportunities for Reflection**: Regularly reviewing your time management practices encourages self-reflection. This introspection helps you to recognize what is truly important to you, leading to more meaningful choices and greater fulfillment.

Mastering time management cultivates a structured approach to life that alleviates stress, enhances focus, and fosters a sense of control.

The result is not just improved productivity, but a profound sense of peace of mind that allows you to enjoy both your successes and your personal life.

By investing in your time management skills, you invest in your mental well-being and overall happiness.

Achieving Peace of Mind in Life, Business, and Sports with a Balanced Life

To cultivate a sense of peace of mind in life and business, it is essential to balance work, leisure, and personal development. Establishing boundaries is crucial, allowing individuals to devote adequate time and energy to various aspects of their lives.

This balance in sports translates into maintaining physical fitness while supporting mental well-being. Regular physical activity helps alleviate stress, fosters discipline and enhances performance. Additionally, prioritizing mental health through mindfulness practices and self-reflection can significantly impact decision-making and interpersonal relationships within business and sports environments. Ultimately, embracing a holistic approach that combines work, recreation, and self-care paves the way for a fulfilling and peaceful life.

Achieving a balanced lifestyle between business, life, and sports may seem challenging, but it is possible with the right strategies. You can lead a more fulfilling and satisfying life by setting clear boundaries, prioritizing self-care, and making time for loved ones. Remember, balance is not about perfection but finding harmony in everyday activities.

Chapter 47

The Pursuit of "Peace of Mind" Success in Life, Business, and Sports

According to legendary basketball coach John Wooden, ***"Success is peace of mind, knowing you have done your best to become the best you are capable of becoming."***

This chapter explores how this profound definition of success applies to sports and the broader canvas of life and business. We'll draw on personal anecdotes, such as my own journey in sports and business, and lessons from sports figures to illuminate how striving to achieve one's best can lead to genuine fulfillment and *peace of mind*.

Defining Success Beyond Winning

The Wooden Philosophy

John Wooden, revered as one of the greatest coaches in sports history, led UCLA to ten NCAA national championships in 12 years, including an unprecedented seven in a row. However, Wooden's philosophy of success was more than just winning games. He believed sincerely in the process of self-improvement and personal excellence. Wooden's famous "Pyramid of Success" highlights attributes like industriousness, enthusiasm, friendship, loyalty, and cooperation as foundational blocks. According to Wooden, achieving success means excelling in the process and effort, regardless of the outcome. This approach underscores that success is about self-satisfaction and inner peace, derived from the knowledge that you gave everything you had.

Personal Story: John Wooden's Legacy

One of the most poignant stories about Wooden's philosophy comes from his reflections. Wooden often recounted how he never spoke to his teams about winning. Instead, he emphasized preparation and the importance of doing their best. His focus was always on the effort, not the score. This mindset led his teams to remarkable achievements. Yet, Wooden maintained that his proudest moments were not the championships but his players' personal growth and development, a testament to the transformative power of his approach.

Lessons from Sports to Life

1. The Importance of Preparation

Preparation is not just a key to success, it's the master key. Athletes spend countless hours training, strategizing, and perfecting their skills. This lesson is equally applicable to life. Whether it's preparing for a presentation at work, studying for an exam, or planning a family event, thorough preparation often determines the outcome. Success is not a single moment of triumph but the culmination of consistent, dedicated effort.

2. Resilience in the Face of Adversity

Sports teach us a valuable lesson in resilience. Athletes frequently face setbacks, from injuries to losses, yet they learn to bounce back, stronger and more determined. Resilience is not just a trait, it's a mindset. It's equally important in life. Challenges and failures are inevitable, but our ability to recover and move forward defines our true success.

3. The Power of Teamwork

No athlete achieves greatness alone. Teamwork is integral to sports, emphasizing collaboration, trust, and mutual support. Similarly, our relationships and networks play a critical role in our success. Surrounding ourselves with supportive people and working collectively towards common goals enhances our chances of achieving personal and professional success.

4. Integrity and Character

Sports instill values of honesty, fairness, and sportsmanship. Winning at all costs is not the goal; it's about playing the game with integrity and respect. In life, these values are equally significant. Acting with integrity and maintaining strong moral principles earns respect and trust, foundational to long-term success.

5. Continuous Improvement

Athletes are always looking to improve, no matter their level of success. They analyze their performances, seek feedback, and make adjustments. This mindset of continuous improvement is vital in life. We should always strive to learn, grow, and enhance our skills and knowledge, aiming to be better today than yesterday.

Applying These Lessons

Practical Steps for Everyday Success

1. **Set Clear Goals**: Define what success means to you. Set specific, achievable goals that align with your values and aspirations.

2. **Create a Plan**: Develop a roadmap to achieve your goals. Break your larger goals into smaller, manageable tasks.

3. **Stay Consistent**: Consistency is critical. Put in the effort every day, even when progress seems slow.

4. **Seek Feedback**: Be open to feedback and use it to improve. Constructive criticism is a tool for growth.

5. **Build a Support Network**: Surround yourself with people who motivate and support you. Collaboration often leads to more significant achievements.

6. **Reflect and Adjust**: Regularly reflect on your progress and make necessary adjustments to stay on track.

Achieving Peace of Mind Through Success in Business, Life, and Sports

Success is not merely a destination but a continuous journey of self-improvement and personal excellence. By adopting the principles learned from sports—preparation, resilience, teamwork, integrity, and continuous improvement—we can achieve a profound sense of fulfillment and peace of mind in all areas of life.

It's important to remember that success in one area should not come at the expense of others. Balancing our personal and professional lives is crucial for a holistic sense of fulfillment and peace of mind.

John Wooden's legacy teaches us that success lies in the effort and commitment to becoming the best we can be. By focusing on this internal success metric, we can lead more meaningful, satisfying lives.

The Essence of Peace of Mind

Peace of mind is not the absence of challenges or the elimination of external chaos—it is the deep and unshakable calm that comes from within. It is the quiet confidence that arises when we align ourselves with our values, embrace the present moment, and release the need to control the uncontrollable.

True peace of mind is a balance—a harmony between acceptance and action, between letting go and holding on. It is the courage to face uncertainty with grace and the wisdom to find joy in the simple, fleeting moments of life.

As we navigate the complexities of existence, peace of mind becomes not just a fleeting emotion but a practice—a way of being. It is cultivated through patience, self-awareness, empathy, and trust in the unfolding of life. It teaches us that while we cannot always change what happens to us, we can always choose how we respond.

In the end, peace of mind is the quiet assurance that, no matter the storm, we have the strength to endure and the clarity to cherish what truly matters. It is a gift we give ourselves and those around us—a state of being that transcends fear and fosters love, connection, and meaning. May we all strive to nurture this profound sense of inner serenity, allowing it to guide us through life with purpose and compassion.

www.ingramcontent.com/pod-product-compliance
Lightning Source LLC
Chambersburg PA
CBHW070048080526
44586CB00013B/968